M

Saint-Michel

from **A** *to* **Z**

Henry Decaëns
Adrien Goetz
Gérard Guillier
Maylis Baylé

Translated by
John and Véronique Wood

Flammarion

SOME QUESTIONS ...

An immense bay; dramatic tides as celebrated as they are treacherous; a mighty rocky outcrop; remarkable fauna and flora; an unparalleled setting – the Mont is first and foremost a miracle of nature. But what can be done to rescue it from the threat of the encroaching sands?

Under the protection of Saint Michael, the abbey was one of the most important in Normandy throughout the Middle Ages. To what did it owe its spiritual and cultural prestige? Why does it remain one of the most visited sites in Europe today?

By the time the Mont was listed as a historic monument, restoration its had become a matter of the greatest urgency. The work of restoring the buildings has gone on for generations. Each had its specific function. How can this be recovered and respected at such a distance in time?

... AND ANSWERS

Visitor's Guide p. 6

The Visitor's Guide presents an overall picture of Mont-Saint-Michel, drawing together the articles which appear in the A *to* Z Section under three thematic and historical headings, each with its own colour code.

■ The site:
the abbey,
the town,
the bay.

▦ Its inhabitants:
monks,
defenders,
builders.

■ The context:
the historical
background,
artistic styles.

The information given in each article, together with the cross-references indicated by asterisks and the numbers in brackets which refer to the general plan, will enable the reader to explore the guide – and the site – at leisure.

A *to* Z Section p. 29

Arranged in alphabetical order, the articles of the A *to* Z Section contain everything the visitor needs to know in order to enter the world of Mont-Saint-Michel. They are complemented by detailed descriptions of the principal sites, and by highlighted panels surveying the historical and artistic background against which the architecture of the Mont has evolved.

The story of Mont-Saint-Michel p. 11

The guide opens with a brief history of Mont-Saint-Michel, setting it in its context and developing the main themes and topics set out in the A *to* Z Section.

I. THE GENESIS OF THE SITE

A. Formation of the bay

An immense bay swept by the strongest tides in Europe: from this vast flat expanse bordered by the headlands of Champeaux and Le Grouin rise Mont-Saint-Michel, Tombelaine and Mont-Dol. Originally part of the mainland, these three rocky outcrops became islands following a rise in sea level brought about by a warming of the climate.

- *Bay*
- *Chausey (Isles of)*
- *Couesnon (River)*
- *Earth Tremors*
- *Geology of the site*
- *Mont-Dol*
- *Tides*
- *Tombelaine*

B. Silting

'Mont-Saint-Michel must remain an island,' wrote Victor Hugo in the nine-teenth century. The construction of the causeway and the reclaiming of pold-ers for agriculture have endangered its maritime character, however : with each tide yet more sediment accumulates in the bay.

- *Fauna and flora*
- *Island Character*
- *Polders*
- *Silting in the bay*

C. Perils of the bay

Although it may not reach 'the speed of a galloping horse', the tide can come in extremely quickly and has taken more than a few imprudent wanderers by surprise. Sea mists and quicksands are equally treacherous hazards in the bay.

- *Quicksands*
- *Tides*

II. THE AGE OF THE MONKS

A. A centre of pilgrimage

From the sixth century there were hermits living on Mont-Saint-Michel. In the early eighth century Aubert, Bishop of Avranches, built a shrine there in honour of Saint Michael, who had appeared to him in a vision. The arrival of a community of twelve canons was to transform the Mont into a great centre of pilgrimage.

- *Aubert (Saint)*
- *Legends*
- *Michael (Saint)*
- *Middle Ages*
- *Mont-Tombe*
- *Norman Invasions*
- *Pilgrimages*

B. 'City of books'

Under the influence of Richard II Duke of Normandy, the Mont's reputation as a place of worship and pilgrimage became firmly established. As a centre of loyalty to the Norman cause, the Mont became increasingly wealthy. The construction of Notre-Dame-sous-Terre was followed by a succession of new buildings which transformed the modest sanctuary into a thriving abbey, dubbed the 'city of books'.

- *Abbey Church*
- *Aquilon Chamber*
- *Benedictine Order*
- *Construction*
- *Crypts*
- *Dormitory*
- *Dungeons*
- *Infirmary*
- *Manuscripts*
- *Normandy*
- *Notre-Dame-sous-Terre*
- *Promenoir (Monks' Gallery)*

C. The 'Merveille'

During the war between Philippe Auguste and the Duke of Normandy, Mont-Saint-Michel was put to the torch. In order to make reparation, the king donated a substantial sum of money which was to fund building work on the Merveille. Complemented by the charter room, guardroom and Belle-Chaise, this architectural ensemble is one of the jewels of Gothic architecture.

- *Almonry*
- *Belle-Chaise*
- *Brittany*
- *Chapter House*
- *Charter Room*
- *Cloister*
- *Guardroom*
- *Guest Chamber*
- *Knights' Chamber*
- *Merveille*
- *Refectory*
- *Storeroom*

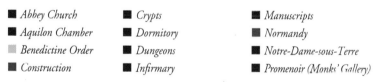

III. THE DEFENCE OF THE CITADEL

A. Facing English attack

During the Hundred Years War the Mont became a fortress. The entrance to the village was protected by powerful ramparts, and the abbey was defended by an impressive redoubt known as the Châtelet. These fortifications, a garrison of knights and the protection afforded by the sea enabled the citadel to remain in French hands, even when the English occupied nearby Tombelaine.

- *Abbey Lodgings*
- *Châtelet*
- *Cisterns*
- *Du Guesclin (Bertrand)*
- *Forward Gate*
- *Hundred Years War*
- *Jolivet (Robert)*
- *King's Gate and Tower*
- *Ramparts*
- *Watch-dogs*

B. The Bastille of the sea

After the war, Abbot Guillaume d'Estouteville rebuilt the chancel of the abbey church and brought new vigour to the abbey. The kings of France came on pilgrimage to the Mont once more. In 1469, Louis XI created the Order of Saint Michel. The abbey, meanwhile, started to receive its first prisoners.

- *Chancel*
- *Estouteville (Guillaume d')*
- *Gabriel (Tower)*
- *Iron cage*
- *Lace Staircase*
- *Order of Saint-Michel*
- *Royal Visits*

C. A resurgence of monasticism

The absentee abbots of the sixteenth century merely exploited the abbey's revenues. The monastic rule became increasingly lax and building works ceased. After the Wars of Religion, the monastery's spiritual vocation was restored to it by the monks of the Congregation of Saint Maur. By the end of the eighteenth century, however, the community was too small to maintain the abbey.

- *Commendatary Abbots*
- *Congregation of Saint Maur*
- *Wars of Religion*
- *West Terrace*

IV. 'A TOAD IN A RELIQUARY'

A. The prison

At the Revolution the monks were forced to abandon the abbey. In 1793 there began the darkest period in the history of the Mont. Refractory priests, common prisoners and political detainees were sent to this state prison, reviled by Hugo in 1836. Only in 1863 was the prison shut down.

■ *Prison*   ▨ *Writers and Fiction*
■ *Wheel (Great)*

B. An exemplary restoration

The abbey was classified as a historic monument in 1874. Through the work of architects of the Monuments Historiques, the Mont rose from its ruins to become a site of increasing renown. In 1893-7, Victor Petitgrand rebuilt the central tower and added an elegant steeple, thus restoring the monument's tall and slender profile.

▨ *Architects*   ■ *Historic Monument*   ■ *Steeple*
■ *Fanils*   ▨ *Painters*   ▨ *Viollet-le-Duc*

C. An international reputation

Since that time, the Mont has attracted visitors in ever increasing numbers. Now recognized as a world heritage site by UNESCO, Mont-Saint-Michel is one of France's most prestigious monuments. The abbey nevertheless remains a place of prayer, thanks to the presence of a small religious community installed in the abbey lodgings in 1969.

■ *Causeway*   ■ *Parish Church*   ▨ *Poulard (Mère)*
■ *Commerce*   ■ *Tourism*
■ *Community*   ■ *UNESCO*
▨ *Frémiet (Emmanuel)*   ■ *Village*

THE STORY OF MONT-SAINT-MICHEL

Mont-Saint-Michel and its breathtaking bay have always exercised a powerful attraction. Home to both a famous pilgrimage centre and a thriving Benedictine abbey, it has a long history closely intertwined with that of Normandy and France. Constructed as a place of prayer for monks and of welcome for pilgrims, the magnificent buildings crowning the rock trace the evolution of Romanesque and Gothic architecture, and together constitute a unique testimony to the civilization of the Middle Ages.

I. The genesis of the site
A. Formation of the bay

Mont-Saint-Michel owes its fame partly to the 40,000-hectare bay* from which it rises. Three small coastal rivers – the Sée, Sélune, and Couesnon* – flow into it, tracing wide meanders which (on the uncanalized sections) change course with the tides. Frequently land, sea and sky dissolve together into a uniform slate-grey haze.

The bay is raked by the strongest tides to be found anywhere in Europe, with a difference between consecutive high and low water levels sometimes exceeding fifteen metres. At low tide the sea often disappears over the horizon, some twenty kilometres away, leaving a great expanse of calcareous clay and sand, known locally as *tangue*, around Mont-Saint-Michel and the islet of Tombelaine,* three kilometres to the north.

Composed of granulite, an extremely hard crystalline rock, these two rocky outcrops were thrust upwards through the layer of schist which covers the floor of the bay. During the last ice age, 10,000 years ago, the sea level was lower, and the Mont was surrounded by the forest which gave rise to the legend* of the forest of Scissy. Rather than being swept away by a tidal wave supposedly caused by an earth tremor,* the forest was submerged by a rise in sea level following a period of global warming some 8,000 years ago (see Island).

B. Silting

Since that time, the bay has been subject to a constant process of silting,* a natural phenomenon caused by the incoming tide depositing more silt than the ebb tide removes. Over the last century and a half it has been aggravated, however, by man-made reclamation schemes designed to create polders.* The companies authorized to carry out these schemes in 1856 embarked upon a huge operation to prevent the rivers from meandering as they crossed the bay, canalizing the Couesnon from the bend at Moidrey as far as Mont-Saint-Michel,

The bay seen from Mont-Saint-Michel.

and constructed a sub-tidal causeway from la Roche-Torin, six kilometres east of the Mont. This was followed a few years later by the dry causeway* linking the Mont to the mainland, built by the state. With the rivers brought under control, it was then possible gradually to extend the dykes, which now protect almost 3,000 hectares of polders.

It would be a simple matter today to reclaim more land, as the sea deposits between a million and a million and a half cubic metres of sediment in the bay every year. When the sands reach a level of twelve to thirteen metres above low water, moreover, they are covered only by exceptionally high tides, and consequently become host to a carpet of salt-loving plants which stabilize the silt. These salt meadows are the famous *prés salés*, grazed by sheep whose meat is particularly prized (see Fauna and Flora).

But the Mont remains inseparable from its maritime location, and for this reason it is essential to continue the struggle against the process of silting, principally by carrying out the necessary work to allow the tides and coastal rivers to sweep the sands freely once more.

View of the western side of Mont-Saint-Michel.

C. Perils of the bay

Although the bay may appear welcoming, tempting walkers on to its sands, its exceptional tides make it perilous. The sea surges into the bay on an incoming tide at an average speed of 3.750 kilometres per hour, which is already appreciable, and in certain places and at certain times it can move considerably faster. Another danger lies in the sea mist, which can shroud the bay completely in under an hour and is notoriously disorientating.

For many people the most treacherous feature of the bay is its quick-sands,* but it is in fact quite possible for anyone familiar with the sands to avoid them. Conversely, it is not always easy to spot the deep pools in the river channels scoured out by the turbulent tides.

There is thus nothing mythical about the hazards of the sands. For medieval pilgrims they possessed a spiritual significance, as the perilous crossing of the bay foreshadowed in their eyes the journey of the soul towards heaven, menaced by the Devil but also fortunate enough to be under the protection of the Archangel.

II. The age of the monks
A. A centre of pilgrimage

The early history of the Mont-Saint-Michel has come down to us through a tenth-century chronicle, the *Revelatio ecclesiae sancti Michaelis,* which relates how the Mont was originally called Mont-Tombe.* From the sixth century it was home to a few Christian hermits, who were said to have built two chapels on the rock, one dedicated to Saint Stephen and the other to Saint Symphorien. The *Revelatio* goes on to relate how the cult of the Archangel came to be established on the island. One night in the year 708, a bishop of Avranches named Aubert* had a vision of Saint Michael* in a dream, in which the saint commanded him to build a church in his honour on Mont-Tombe. On his third appearance, impatient with the reluctance of Aubert, who dismissed the dream as illusion, Saint Michael is said to have pierced the prelate's forehead with a beam of light from his forefinger. Thus it

Saint Clément, *Recognitiones. Scriptorium of Mont-Saint-Michel: the copyist Gueldin presents his book to Saint Michael,* tenth century. Avranches, Bibliothèque Municipale (ms 50, fol 1 verso).

was that Saint Aubert built a small oratory, modelled on the sanctuary of Monte Gargano in southern Italy where Saint Michael was said to have appeared in 492. In order to receive the faithful wishing to put themselves under the protection of the Archangel, he put a number of regular canons in charge of the new sanctuary. And so it was that the Mont became one of the greatest centres of pilgrimage* in medieval Christendom, apparently continuing to attract the faithful even during the turbulent times of the Norman* invasions.

B. 'City of books'

The creation of Normandy* in 911 was of little immediate consequence for the Mont, as the Cotentin peninsula was not attached to the new province until 933. The Normans were not slow to realize the importance of the sanctuary lying on the fringes of their territory, however. In 965, Duke Richard II replaced the canons, whose loyalties almost certainly lay too closely with Brittany,* with Benedictine* monks* from the abbey of Saint Wandrille at Fontenelle, whose commitment to Normandy was beyond question. The Mont would henceforth fulfil a double role as pilgrimage centre and Benedictine abbey (see Conventual buildings). The Benedictines were probably responsible for building the church of Notre-Dame-sous-Terre* as well as a pre-Romanesque abbey church on the summit of the Mont. These sanctuaries quickly became too small, as by the start of the eleventh century the community already numbered fifty monks, and the number of pilgrims was growing all the time.

The prosperity subsequently brought to the monastery by pilgrims' offerings and the revenue from its priories* enabled it to embark on the building of a great abbey church* to crown the rock, started in

1023 and finished in 1085 – and therefore not yet completed when Duke William the Bastard (later known as Wiliam the Conqueror*) visited the Mont in 1064. It then became necessary to replace the pre-Romanesque monastery, which was too small, with more spacious conventual buildings. Of these eleventh-century lodgings, redesigned in the following century, there remains the three-storey Romanesque* building on the north flank of the rock, below the level of the church, which contains (in ascending order) the Aquilon Chamber,*

Saint Augustine, *Contra Faustum.* Scriptorium of Mont-Saint-Michel: illuminated capital, 1050-1100. Avranches, Bibliothèque Municipale (ms 90, fol 2 recto).

the Promenoir (Monks' Gallery),* the dormitory* and, to one side, the Romanesque infirmary.

All these buildings, together with those erected to the west and south of Notre-Dame-sous-Terre, were completed under the abbotcy of Robert de Torigni* (1154-86). The first abbot's lodgings, the dungeons,* the chapel of Saint Etienne* and the ossuary* are now virtually all that remains of this great twelfth-century building programme. Not content merely with his architectural achievements, Robert was also a shrewd administrator, a skilful diplomat and a historian: so numerous were the manuscripts* with which he enriched the abbey that it soon became known as the 'city of books'.

Emile Sagot, *Cross-section of the western buildings of the Merveille,* showing (from top to bottom) the cloister, Knights' Chamber and storeroom. Watercoloured drawing. Musée d'Avranches.

C. The 'Merveille'

When Philippe Auguste annexed Normandy to the kingdom of France in 1204, the inhabitants of the Mont, still loyal to King John ('Lackland') of England, came under attack from Breton soldiers allied to the French king. Unable to capture the Mont the Bretons withdrew, but not before starting a fire which reduced part of the abbey to ashes (see Fires). The French king, eager to have this unfortunate exploit on the part of his allies forgotten, is said subsequently to have given money for the restoration of the illustrious abbey. As a result, the monastery did not remain in a ruined state for long, and the lodgings which had burned down were swiftly replaced with the celebrated buildings of the 'Merveille',* built between 1212 and 1228 to the north of the abbey church and using as its foundations the lower section of a twelfth-century building which had partly survived the fire. Its mighty external buttresses emphasizing its giddy height, the Merveille is one of the finest surviving examples of thirteenth-century monastic architecture. It is in fact composed of two separate edifices, built side by side and virtually simultaneously: the older eastern part, containing the almonry,* guest chamber* and refectory,* and the western part containing the storeroom*, Knights' Chamber* and cloister,* placed one above the other.

A plan to erect a third building to the west of the cloister, which would have contained the chapter house,* was finally abandoned, going no further than the provision of a charter room* for the abbey archives in the north-western corner. This was not the end of building works on the Mont, however: in the mid-thirteenth century

Richard Turstin, the first abbot to be accorded the right to wear a bishop's mitre, had a new entrance – the Salle des Gardes or guardroom* – built on the eastern side, with above it the Chamber of Belle-Chaise,* for the fitting administration of ecclesiastical justice.

Following this the abbey was honoured by visits from a number of distinguished pilgrims, including the French kings Louis IX, Philippe III le Hardi (the Bold), and Philippe IV le Bel (the Handsome) (see Royal Visits).

Emile Sagot, *The north façade of the Charter Room.* Watercoloured drawing. Musée d'Avranches.

III. The defence of the citadel
A. Facing English attack

In the late fourteenth century a succession of abbots oversaw the building of the most extensive section of the abbey lodgings,* extending southwards from Belle-Chaise* to complete the labyrinth of buildings surrounding the abbey church. After the start of the Hundred Years War,* however, their attention was to be directed principally to the construction of military defences. Since 1357 the abbots had been titular captains of the garrison, a responsibility which in practice they delegated to a military commander such as Bertrand Du Guesclin* (appointed that same year).

To house the garrison, Pierre Le Roy, abbot from 1386 to 1411, built the tower now named after him. He also fortified the abbey entrance by constructing the Châtelet* in front of it. His successor, Robert Jolivet,* encircled the village with powerful ramparts* before, in 1420 – believing the French cause to be lost – offering his services to the English king. From his new base in Rouen he became an active collaborator with the English regent, the Duke of Bedford, and even helped the English in their attempts to breach the defences with which he himself had equipped the Mont.

Emile Sagot, *Mont-Saint-Michel: projected restoration of the ramparts.* Watercoloured drawing. Musée d'Avranches.

Overleaf: Chancel of the abbey church.

Happily the Mont withstood their attacks, beoming the only part of Normandy to remain loyal to the French king.

For a number of years the position of the rock was extremely precarious: in 1419 the English had succeeded in capturing the islet of Tombelaine, which they held until 1450. Protected by the sea, by which it was surrounded more frequently than it is today, and defended by 119 valiant knights under their captain Louis d'Estouteville, who perfected the island's defences, the Mont nevertheless managed to hold out against the English.

B. The Bastille of the sea

On the death of Jolivet in 1444, Guillaume d'Estouteville,* brother of the captain, was appointed to the abbotcy on the initiative of Charles VII. The beginning of his term of office coincided with the end of the Hundred Years War, heralding a new era of prosperity for

the abbey and its pilgrimage centre, and making possible the rebuilding in Flamboyant Gothic* style of the chancel* of the abbey church, which had collapsed in 1421.

Henceforth the Mont became a symbol of victory over the English, and the great figures of the kingdom of France made a point of coming to give thanks to Saint

Arms of the abbey of Mont-Saint-Michel, on the south side of the nave of the abbey church.

Michael. Louis XI himself came on pilgrimage three times, in 1462,1467 and 1473. On his first visit he granted the abbey the privilege of adding three gold fleurs-de-lis azure to its coat of arms of three sable escallops argent. In 1469, at the château of Amboise, he created the Order of Saint Michel* as a token of his faith. Sadly he was also responsible for installing a state prison in the Romanesque buildings, containing one of the notorious iron cages* invented by Cardinal La Balue. Thus the monastery earned the unfortunate sobriquet of 'Bastille of the sea'.

C. A resurgence of monasticism

As in other monasteries, the Benedictine rule gradually became increasingly lax on the Mont. Matters became worse after 1516 with the institution of the commendatary system, by which the abbot was no longer elected by the community, as stipulated by the rule, but was appointed by the king. These absentee commendatary abbots* entrusted the spiritual welfare of the community to a prior – a disastrous arrangement, as the abbot was intended to be the cornerstone of the whole Benedictine system. On the material level the abbey scarcely fared any better, as the abbots were concerned less with the upkeep of the buildings than with disposing of the revenues. After the completion of the chancel of the church in 1521, no significant building work was undertaken. The turmoil of the Wars of Religion* did nothing to restore order to the monasteries. The Mont narrowly escaped being pillaged by Protestant forces under Montgomery, but only at the cost of a terrible massacre of the Huguenots in 1591.

Happily the decline was halted for several decades by the monks of the Congregation of Saint Maur,* who settled on the Mont in 1622, bringing with them a renewed emphasis on the spiritual life of the community as well as on scholarship. Two of their number, Dom Jean Huynes and Dom Thomas Le Roy, wrote a history of the Mont – a work which is all the more precious today following the destruction of the original archives by fire at Saint-Lô (Manche) in 1944.

Sadly the beneficial effects of these reforms faded with time. By the end of the eighteenth century the community numbered barely a dozen monks who, unable to restore the first three bays of the church which were on the point of collapse, were forced to pull them down (see West Terrace).

IV. 'A toad in a reliquary'
A. The prison

During the Revolution monastic vows were abolished and the property of the Church was nationalized, forcing the monks to abandon the abbey in 1790. The buildings did not remain empty for long, however. From May 1793 they became a prison,* receiving as their first batch of inmates over three hundred priests who had refused to accept their enforced civilian status. Breton royalist rebels – the Chouans – and common criminals were later to join them in the freezing, damp cells. Decrees of 6 June 1811 and 2 April 1817 designated the abbey officially as a 'house of detention', and over six hundred common law prisoners were soon to be crammed within its walls. Under the July

Armand Barbès in his cell. Engraving.

21

Monarchy part of the monastery was even used to imprison political detainees, including notably Barbès and Blanqui.

Men of letters were the first to protest against this sacrilegious practice: 'A toad in a reliquary. When, I ask, will the people of this country understand the sanctity of its monuments?', stormed Victor Hugo in 1836. Eventually, in 1863, these protests bore fruit, and Napoleon III ordered the closure of the prison, which ironically had helped to safeguard the buildings, as some, like Arcisse de Caumont, were bold enough to acknowledge: 'It were better [...] to see the Mont-Saint-Michel occupied by thieves than to see it abandoned.'

B. An exemplary restoration

Mgr Bravard, Bishop of Coutances and Avranches, was determined to bring the abbey back to life again. In 1865 he rented the buildings, installing in them diocesan missionaries who were to stay until 1886. They set about the initial work of cleaning the abbey by removing all the extraneous constructions added by the prison administration. The entire fabric of the monument was in a poor state, however, urgently requiring a more fundamental approach caried out by specialists, notably the architects* of the Historic Monuments* service. The first to be appointed was Edouard Corroyer in 1872; two years later the abbey was officially classified as a historic monument and was thus assured of effective protection.

Massive restoration works requiring the deployment of tremendous resources followed, the most spectacular being the rebuilding of the church's central tower in 1893-7, complete with a timbered roof and steeple.*

Radical interventions such as this have nevertheless remained the exception. Architects working on the Mont have generally been more conservative

Restoration of the eastern passage of the cloisters by the 'Monuments Historiques', c.1880.

Overleaf:
Emile Eugène Isabey
(1804-86),
The Mont in a Storm (detail).
Oil on canvas.
Amiens, Musée de Picardie.

André Milaire, poster for the State Railways, 1922. Paris, private collection.

in their approach, making every effort to respect and preserve as far as possible all the original features of the monument, and thus contributing to a restoration scheme which may be considered exemplary.

C. An international reputation

The purpose of the missionaries' stay on the Mont was to revive the custom of pilgrimage and encourage the cult of Saint Michael. On 3 July 1877 a statue of the Archangel, now in the parish church,* was crowned during a grandiose ceremony attended by eleven prelates, over 1200 priests, and 25,000 pilgrims. When the authorities terminated the missionaries' lease in 1886, the cult of the Archangel was transferred to the parish church. The construction of the causeway giving access to the Mont in 1879 and the opening of a railway along it in 1901 encouraged the growth of pilgrimages. This in turn encouraged the church to organize celebrations in 1908-9 to commemorate the twelfth centenary of the religious foundation on the Mont.

This new ease of access to the Mont also attracted increasing numbers of visitors: from a mere 10,000 in 1860 they swelled to 30,000 annually from around 1885, after the construction of the causeway, and in 1910, a few years after the opening of the railway, reached 100,000. Local commerce* also enjoyed a new-found prosperity, famously symbolized by Mère Poulard.

Today two and a half million visitors pass through the village gates every year, and thirty per cent of these climb up to the summit of the rock to visit the abbey. For many of them it is more than a work of art. Indeed, to celebrate the thousandth anniversary of the arrival of Benedictines on the Mont, monks returned here for a few months of 1965 and 1966. In 1969 the authorities gave permission for a permanent community* to be established in the abbey lodgings. Following the example of their medieval forebears, the members of this small community devote themselves to welcoming all who wish to pray and meditate in this marvellous place.

Henry DECAËNS

The abbey church, detail of the timber vault over the nave and the clerestory windows.

◼ Abbey Church

Construction of the abbey church was started in 1023 by Abbot Hildebert to replace its predecessor built by Abbot Maynard, destroyed by fire.* The chancel and transepts were finished before 1058, and the nave, completed in the last thirty years of the eleventh century, was quickly restored after the destruction of the north side, which collapsed in 1103. The Romanesque* chevet, depicted in one of the illuminations of the Duc de Berry's *Très Riches Heures,* collapsed in 1421 and was rebuilt in the second half of the fifteenth century (see Chancel). It stood over a crypt* and comprised an ambulatory of polygonal design without chapels.

A regular crossing is flanked by transepts built over deep vaulted crypts and possessing shallow apsidioles let into their eastern sides. Consisting of two storeys, they are covered, unusually for Normandy, by a barrel vault, attributed to Raoul who died in 1058. The three-storey nave probably remains as intended in 1023, at least on its southern side: its second storey is quite plain, consisting of a series of low twin bays contained beneath relieving arches which recall those of the abbey church at Bernay, but whose surface displays a more highly developed sense of modelling. On the south side of the nave lofty arches rise the full height of all three storeys. The first three bays of the nave, demolished in the eighteenth century by the Maurists (see Congregation of Saint Maur), stood on the site occupied by the platform of the West Terrace.* Excavations have uncovered a vast porch of massive construction which preceded the nave. The present façade dates from around 1780 and was restored in about 1858.

With its ambulatory and massive porch, the building conforms to a pattern typical of Norman architecture before 1050, recalling the chevets of Jumièges, Saint-Wandrille and Avranches, as well as the massive west ends of Jumièges and La Trinité at Caen in its original state.

The greater part of this church underwent very extensive restoration in the nineteenth century and at the beginning of the twentieth, carried out by Victor Petitgrand and Paul Gout (see Architects; Steeple). MB

The abbey church, view of the interior.

24 Abbey Lodgings

The abbey lodgings, dating from the thirteenth to the fifteenth centuries, lie on the southern flank of the Mont, in a tall and precipitous complex whose curved façade forms a sort of enclosure in front of the abbey church.*

The abbot was responsible for the material organization of his monastery, for hospitality to guests, for pilgrimages* and for management of the abbeys numerous estates. To accommodate these services and their staff, lay buildings were constructed alongside the upper section of the Grand Degré.* Near the entrance was the Belle-Chaise* – the abbot's court room – then the bailiff's offices where civil and judicial affairs were dealt with by a bailiff representing the abbot. Other rooms housed the abbey's administrative and legal departments. Soon afterwards, in the fourteenth century, the abbot's quarters were built beside these buildings. Laid out on three levels, they have all the appearance of a palace, reflecting the rise in social position of abbots generally, and particularly on the Mont, where the abbot was often a friend and counsellor of the powerful figures of the day.

Over the following centuries, successive additions were to give the building its final, majestic profile. GG

31 Almonry

The almonry, along with the storeroom* which communicates with it, is in the Romanesque style. The greater part of these two rooms belonged to a twelfth-century building, the bottom floor of which was retained when the Merveille* was built.

The almonry is a fine room of considerable proportions, thirty-five metres long and divided into two aisles by a central row of columns of alternate full and half-drums. Their smooth and unadorned capitals support a continuous groined vault with no subdivisions.

Everything is simple in this room, where the monks welcomed the poor as they had formerly done in the Aquilon Chamber.* Various practical arrangements included a hoist allowing food prepared in the kitchen near the monks' refectory* to be sent down, and two chutes built into the splayed window openings for the disposal of rubbish. HD

Southern façade of the abbey lodgings.

The almonry, detail of column and groined vault.

29 Aquilon Chamber

The Aquilon Chamber is a fine example of eleventh-century Romanesque architecture.* Little restored, it has retained much of its original appearance. Sited on the north-west flank of the rock, it served as the foundation for the Romanesque monastic buildings constructed vertically on top of it. Directly above it lay the Promenoir* or Monks' Gallery, and above that again the monks' dormitory.* Its name derives from its position facing the chill northerly wind known as the 'Aquilon', and it was here that the poor would be offered food and shelter. Today the plan of the room is rectangular. In the centre, two granite columns topped with sturdy carved capitals support the springers of rounded and broken Romanesque arches. The groined vaulting, also Romanesque, is in a perfect state of preservation. Nine centuries later, traces of the planks used to shore up the masonry during construction* work can still be seen.GG

Architects

After the prison* was closed in 1863, the abbey required extensive retoration work, carried out by the architects of the 'Monuments Historiques'. The first was Edouard Corroyer, responsible for conservation of the Mont from 1872 to 1888. Although he also worked to consolidate the Romanesque

Opposite:
The Aquilon Chamber.

Edouard Corroyer, *Mont-Saint-Michel, plan for general restoration: north-south cross-section, 1876.* Watercoloured drawing. Musée d'Avranches.

buildings and the ramparts* of the village,* his main preoccupation was the saving of the third level of the Merveille,* including the cloister* and refectory.* The name of Victor Petitgrand, who succeeded him from 1889 to 1898, is associated with the reconstruction of the tower over the crossing of the abbey church, to which he added an elegant steeple.*

From 1898 to 1923, Paul Gout oversaw numerous projects within the abbey buildings and in the village, most notably the complete restoration of the abbey church and four rooms on the first two levels of the Merveille.* He also rebuilt the Grand Degré* or monumental outer stairway, which had crumbled away, and renovated the abbey cisterns.* In 1910 he published a monograph which remains a standard work on the subject.

Pierre Paquet (1923-8) and Bernard Haubold (1929-33) dedicated their efforts to protecting the Mont's surroundings and the site itself. Ernest Herpe (1933-57) restored the complex of abbey lodgings,* and Yves-Marie Froidevaux (1957-83) reopened Notre-Dame-sous-Terre,* re-established the cloister garden and softened some of the rather heavy-handed restoration work carried out previously. His successor, Pierre-André Lablaude, now continues the work of conserving and restoring this monumental site. HD

■ Architecture

Architecture is the means by which for many centuries men have established a concrete relationship with their environment. At Mont-Saint-Michel this relationship is one of exceptional richness.

The architecture of the Mont tells its own story, from pre-Romanesque through Romanesque, Gothic and late Gothic to Flamboyant Gothic. The difficulties presented by the site, particularly the steep rocky slopes of the Mont itself, are a clear indication in themselves of the determination of the builders, who also had to face fire,* earth tremors* and war.* They also bear witness to the tripartite society of the Middle Ages,* in which the military, laity and clergy and their buildings coexisted together.

Architecture is a framework for a way of life. On the Mont, the complex functioning of this huge site was governed by a carefully organized use of space. The architectural surroundings, like any other work of art, possess in addition a spiritual dimension: each structure has its own meaning, and is imbued with its own spirit and atmosphere.

Architecture may also serve a symbolic role. The breathtaking sight of this great architectural pyramid, standing between sea and sky, is a reminder that for centuries the Mont was one of the great spiritual centres of Europe. GG

'A visit to Mont-Saint-Michel offers the same sort of pleasure as one experiences ... when looking through those strange etchings by Piranesi in which he has scratched into the dark varnish his nightmarish architectural visions.'

Théophile Gautier, 1865.

17 Aubert (Saint)

The *Revelatio ecclesiae sancti Michaelis,* a Benedictine* chronicle written in the tenth century, relates how Saint Michael the Archangel came to be honoured on the Mont-Tombe,* as the Mont was then called. One night in the year 708, he appeared in a dream to Saint Aubert, Bishop of Avranches, commanding him to build an oratory in his honour on the rock. The dream had to be repeated three times before the incredulous priest was convinced, whereupon he

The Chapel of
Saint Aubert.

built an oratory modelled on the sanctuary of Monte Gargano on the plain of Puglia in southern Italy, which had been built into a natural grotto where Saint Michael was supposed to have appeared in 492. To serve the new sanctuary, he founded a community of regular canons, who looked after this centre of pilgrimage* until they were replaced by the Benedictines in 966.

A few traces of this primitive oratory have been unearthed behind the south altar of Notre-Dame-sous-Terre.* The chapel of Saint Aubert, at the foot of the Mont, was built in the fifteenth century on a rock which a child was supposed to have rolled down from the top in order to make space for the building of the first sanctuary. The well beside it marks the spot where Saint Aubert is said miraculously to have caused a spring to appear. HD

1 Avancée

See Forward Gate

8 Basse (Tower)

See Ramparts

35

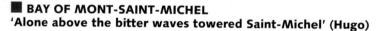

■ BAY OF MONT-SAINT-MICHEL
'Alone above the bitter waves towered Saint-Michel' (Hugo)

The sands around Mont-Saint-Michel furnish the monument with its back-drop of fantasy and myth: drownings, disappearances in the quicksands,* miraculous crossings and a tide* which comes in at the speed of a galloping horse. From the panoramic viewpoint of the botanical gardens in Avranches and the Gué de l'Épine or the Bec d'Andaine at Genêt, from where today's pil-grimages* set out on foot, the Mont can be seen alone in the bay. When the tides run high, it is not difficult to imagine the Archangel's struggles with the forces of evil.

Along a hundred kilometres of coastline – including 'the most beautiful kilo-metre in France', overlooking the cliffs of Champeaux – there has developed a natural environment which is unique of its kind, modified and enriched by the daily tides which, in this largely flat region, inundate an unusually large area. Above the foreshore of sand and mudflats, crossed by the rivers Sée, Sélune and Couesnon,* rise the Mont, the island of Tombelaine* and, away on the coastline, Mont-Dol* (see Geology of the site).

In different areas the tidal deposits take the form of sandy beaches – such as at the resorts of Saint-Pair and Jullouville facing the isles of Chausey* – or of grassland fringed by sand dunes covered with privet and furze. Banks of shells left by *hermelles* (sabellae or peacock-worms) stand out against mudflats criss-crossed by channels in which it is easy to sink into the slimy silt known locally as *tangue*. This area and its landscapes, as well as its characteristic plants and wildlife (see Fauna and Flora), are now threatened by the silting* up of the bay. AG

7 Béatrix (Tower)

See Ramparts

43 Belle-Chaise

In the thirteenth century the abbot, as feudal lord, was responsible for the administration of justice. Accordingly, Abbot Richard Turstin built an official chamber for ecclesiastical and judicial hearings. Situated above the guardroom,* close to the new entrance of the abbey,* it communicated with the Châtelet,* the abbey lodgings* and the Crypte* des Gros Piliers. The room acquired its present name in the late fourteenth century, when Abbot Pierre Le Roy had an exceptionally fine throne installed here.

It is a well-lit chamber, with pairs of windows set into deep bays along its sides and four long, narrow windows looking out to the south-east, and was heated by a large and simple fireplace.

The timbers of the magnificent roof were entirely renewed in 1994 by the architect* Pierre-André Lablaude; embellished with carved and moulded tie-beams and king-posts, it is lined with panelling bearing Gothic arch designs decorated with black fleurs-de-lis, and still showing traces of red and white paint. HD

Opposite:
The bay of Mont-Saint-Michel.

The Belle-Chaise Chamber before the restoration of 1994.

Aretino Spinello, *Saint Benedict of Nursia... at Monte Cassino* (detail), *c.*1400. Fresco. Florence, Church of San Miniato.

■ BENEDICTINE ORDER
Work, prayer and study

In 966, a century before the victory of William the Conqueror* at Hastings, Richard I, Duke of Normandy, sent for twelve Benedictine monks from the abbey of Saint Wandrille at Fontenelle. They were to live on the Mont as the spiritual successors to the twelve canons installed in the first oratory, built on the Mont-Tombe* in 709, with Maynard as the first abbot.

Following donations from the dukes, the Mont became the centre of a vast estate extending well beyond the borders of Normandy.* Later this wealth was to be exploited by the commendatary abbots.*

The rule instituted by Saint Benedict of Nursia (*c.*480-547), which provided for a perfect balance between manual work, prayer and study, was to extend its influence throughout Europe. Indeed the Benedictine order played a considerable part in the development of Christianity in the eleventh and twelfth centuries. The numerous Benedictine priories* and monasteries which sprang up throughout western Christendom, ever faithful to their motto *'Pax'*, fostered an exceptional flowering of culture and the arts which would have not have been possible without their civilizing influence. AG

🔟 Boucle (Tower)
See Ramparts

2 Boulevard
See King's (Gate and Tower)

■ Bourgeois (Guardroom). See Forward Gate

■ Brittany
The marriage of Richard II Duke of Normandy* and Judith of Brittany, celebrated on the Mont between 996 and 1008, could have made the Church of the Archangel a symbol of union between these two powerful dukedoms. It was not destined to be so, however. It was on the Mont that Duke Alain III of Brittany made his public submission to Robert the Magnificent

Antoine du Four, *Lives of Famous Women, Queen Anne of Brittany* (detail), *c.*1505. Nantes, Musée Dobrée.

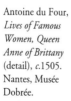

(also known as Robert le Diable, or the Devil), father of William the Conqueror;* and in 1204 the Breton Guy de Thouars, in alliance with Philippe Auguste, invaded the Norman citadel and put it to the torch (see Fires). Brittany has never ceased to play an active part in the history of the Mont, while Normandy has always considered it as its own possession. Bertrand Du Guesclin,* the greatest of all Breton heroes, went so far as to install his wife there. And ten years after her marriage to Charles VIII in 1501, Anne of Brittany, who had inherited the duchy, made a pilgrimage* to the shrine on the Mont, to which the dukes of Brittany often made generous donations. AG

◼ Causeway

The *digue* – a dry causeway built above the tide line between 1877 and 1879 – finally allowed safe access to the Mont after centuries of perilous insecurity; from the turn of the century until the Second World War a steam train set visitors down at the foot of the rock itself. It was also designed to encourage the silting* up of the area, following a course alongside the channel of the Couesnon* and thus preventing the river from flooding and scouring out the eastern part of the bay.* Criticized as an eyesore disfiguring this prestigious site, it aroused considerable opposition even before its construction – carried out in defiance of protests from the ministry responsible for historic monuments and from the press. Controversy continued into the twentieth century, with various plans for its removal, notably in 1914 and in 1937, being abandoned because of the outbreak of war.

In recent years ideas for replacing the causeway have flourished once more, ranging from flattening it to re-routing it or replacing it with a bridge or tunnel, not to mention numerous other 'improvements', such as a string of theme parks or a series of artificial water gardens. Irrespective of their feasibility or advisability, all these propositions make provision for improved access to the Mont, such as increased parking on the mainland and shuttle services for visitors. GG

Arrival of the steam train on the causeway, *c.*1910.

Abbey church, the chancel.

49 Chancel

The chancel, or choir, of the abbey church is one of the most elegant surviving examples of the late Gothic* Flamboyant style. Started in 1446 with the construction of the Crypte* des Gros Piliers, it was not completed until 1521.

Despite the severe restrictions of space, the anonymous architect succeeded in opening up seven chapels off the aisles and ambulatory. Arcade, triforium and clerestory windows are superimposed, their height accentuated by a multiplicity of vertical lines and the tall, narrow proportions of the arches. The main arcade is formed of pillars which are rhomboidal in section, made up of clusters of slender moulded colonnettes, which rise, uninterrupted by capitals, right up into the apex of the arches, some of them soaring twenty-five metres into the vaulting itself. The Flamboyant decoration of the

triforium is of exceptional delicacy, its stone tracery closely
resembling that of Saint-Ouen
in Rouen, on which the chancel
here was almost certainly modelled. As the pillars at this level
were not thick enough to be
pierced, the walkway in the triforium passes behind instead of
through them. Light floods in
through the immensely high
clerestory windows, picking out
the moulding of the surrounding masonry; their mullions,

meanwhile, continue the vertical lines of the triforium, thus
accentuating the soaring quality
of the architecture. No superflu-
ous detail is allowed to detract
from the simplicity of this architectural masterpiece. HD

*'The church possesses a Gothic chancel
and a Romanesque nave, the two
architectural styles vying with each other
in elegance and grandeur.'*

Gustave Flaubert, 1847.

Opposite:
View of the
Châtelet and the
Corbins Tower.

The charter room
at the north-
western corner
of the Merveille.

■ Chapter House

The capitular, or chapter house, was an essential part of the abbey buildings, being the place where the monks* would gather every day to hear a chapter of Saint Benedict's Rule read out, and to take decisions on all important matters affecting the monastery.

The chapter house at the Mont, intended to open onto the western passage of the cloister,* was never built. It is known, however, that in the fifteenth century there were two chapter houses, known as the 'chapter' and the 'little chapter'. The former must have been of substantial size as it was used as a meeting room and occasionally as a refectory, meals being taken in the Merveille* refectory* only on fast days. Because of its vast dimensions and proximity to the Romanesque kitchens just off the Promenoir,* the Knights' Chamber* seems a likely candidate for this role. As for the 'little chapter', a more routine meeting place, it might plausibly have been located in the Promenoir. HD

53 Charter Room

The charter room, in which the charters and documents forming the monastery's archives were kept, was built in 1406 at the north-western corner of the Merveille* by Abbot Pierre le Roy. From the outside it has the appearance of a square tower projecting slightly from the corner of the main building. Internally it consists of two small superimposed rooms, the upper one on a level with the cloister,* the lower one opening into the Knights' Chamber.*

In the eighteenth century, when the library was still intact, the Maurist monk Dom Thomas Le Roy described the lower room as 'vaulted, for the storage of documents and papers kept by the abbot in fine presses and chests which can be seen arranged in admirable order', and the upper room as 'without vaulting, serving as a place for business and the more comfortable perusal of documents and reception of visitors'. GG

20 Châtelet

During the Hundred Years War,* the abbots concentrated their attention on building defences. Pierre Le Roy (1386-

42

1411) raised the Perrine Tower to house the Mont's garrison. In 1393 he fortified the entrance to the abbey with the Châtelet, a narrow construction flanked by two tall corbelled turrets faced with alternate courses of blue and white granite, and crowned with crenellations reaching as far as the Merveille.* The Châtelet gate itself was defended by machicolations, and by a portcullis preventing access to the staircase known as the 'Gouffre' (abyss) which led up to the abbey.

This defensive complex, complemented by a barbican and the Claudine Tower, offered an almost impregnable obstacle to any assailant who might succeed in penetrating the defences of the village* and reaching the top of the Grand Degré* extérieur, or the great outer staircase. HD

■ Chausey (Isles of)

The huge granite outcrop which forms the Chausey archipelago lies some thirty-five kilometres off the coast from Mont-Saint-Michel, from which it can be seen on a clear day. It was in 1022 that Richard II, Duke of Normandy,* presented the abbey with the island of Calsoi, later known as Chausey. When con-

The Isles of Chausey.

struction* of the Romanesque* buildings started, the large island of Chausey was turned into a quarry, with boats ferrying to and fro to keep builders working on the abbey supplied with granite.

The position of the quarry, close to the shore, made loading easier, and the difference between high and low tide (see Tides) provided a convenient means of lifting the huge blocks of stone. Chausey granite continued to be quarried into the twentieth century, and was used notably for the reconstruction of Saint-Malo.

A centre for bird-watchers and a thriving fishing port, Chausey is also a paradise for tourists attracted by this extraordinary seascape, in which hundreds of small islets are continually emerging from the waters only to be swallowed up again by the tides. GG

◼ Cisterns

Cisterns have always played an important part in daily life on the Mont. When the original sanctuary was founded, the small spring known as the 'fontaine Saint-Aubert',* at the foot of the rock's northern face, provided enough water to meet all its needs. Later, as the number of pilgrims* increased, the spring was used exclusively to supply drinking water. For other uses, rainwater was collected in cisterns specially built into the sides of the rock. One such cistern, used to supply water for one of the construction* sites during the twelfth century, was discovered by the architect* Paul Gout beneath the flagstones of the nave.

The sieges of the Hundred Years War* necessitated the provision of more substantial facilities for storing water. In 1417, Abbot Robert Jolivet* had an immense cistern built at the foot of the apse [32]. Hollowed partly out of solid rock, it collected rainwater from the church and the Merveille.* As it was intended to provide drinking water, an ingenious filtering system was incorporated: a well-shaft, perforated at the bottom, was built in the centre of the tank, while the rest of the tank was packed with gravel. Rainwater was then filtered through the gravel before collecting in the central shaft.

Other cisterns were installed in the Crypte* des Gros Piliers, and finally in that of the almonry [56], near the Terrasse du Saut-Gaultier.* Today they form part of the Mont's fire precautions, while drinking water is piped across from the mainland. GG

'From a distance of eight leagues on land and fifteen at sea the Mont-Saint-Michel appears as a vision of the sublime, a marvellous pyramid with steps of mighty rocks fashioned by the ocean, or a high dwelling place carved out by the Middle Ages – a monumental block at whose feet the desert sands of Cheops alternate with the waters of Tenerife.'

Victor Hugo, 1865.

The cloister was a place of silence set aside for meditation and prayer. It also served as a covered passageway, allowing the monks* to come and go between the abbey buildings and the church in all weathers. For this reason the cloister always lies on the same level as the church; on the Mont, where the abbey church* is built on the summit of the rock, this meant that the cloister had to be constructed on the third level of the Merveille,* above the Knights' Chamber.* It communicates only with the refectory* and the dormitory,* since the chapter  house* which should have prolonged the western range was never built.

The delicacy of the cloister stands in marked contrast to the powerful architecture of other parts of the abbey. The walls on the garden side consist of a double row of frail-looking arches, whose colonettes, set in a quincunx pattern linked at the top by diagonal arches, form a series of stable tripods supporting the weight of the roof. The colonettes and their undecorated capitals and circular abacus of English design were largely remade at the end of the nineteenth century, using a fine-grained purple limestone from Lucerne (Manche) very different from the English marble of the original. These slender columns support finely moulded arches between spandrels decorated throughout with carved rosettes and foliage. Here the stonecarvers used fine Caen limestone – soft and easy to work – to give an astonishingly high level of relief to these decorative motifs, typical of Norman work of the thirteenth century. Amid this decor of foliage can be seen a number of carved figures, all of which unfortunately have been badly defaced. One of them depicts Saint Francis of Assisi, who was canonized in 1228, the year in which the cloister was completed.

This elaborate decorative scheme contrasts with the plain granite of the external wall, which is enlivened only by blind arches and spandrels decorated with the incised trefoils so dear to Norman sculptors. In the southern passageway, two arches shelter the benches of the 'mandatum', where the abbot used to wash the feet of twelve monks on Maundy Thursday.

The enclosed garden, replanted in 1965, adds further to the charms of this delightful spot. HD

French eighteenth-
century school,
*Etienne Charles
de Loménie de
Brienne* (detail).
Oil on canvas.
Versailles,
Musée national
du château.

Commendatary Abbots

With the appointment of the thirty-third abbot, Guillaume d'Estouteville* (whose family the king wished to honour) in 1444, and systematically thereafter following the Concordat of Bologna between Francois I and Pope Leo X in 1516, the Mont was confided to abbots chosen by the French king. These abbots, who frequently never took up residence on the Mont, held the abbey *'in commendam'*: in other words, they were responsible for its administration, and – most importantly – were entitled to claim its material 'benefits'.

Thus began a period in which no building was undertaken, the revenues from the abbey and its estates being appropriated for other uses. In 1615, Henri II of Lorraine, future Duc de Guise, was appointed abbot of the Mont when he was only just over a year old. Among his unlikely successors as commendatary abbot were Johann Friedrich de Bebemburg (1703), councillor to the Elector of Bavaria; Charles-Maurice de Broglie (1721) and Loménie de Brienne (1766), finance minister to Louis XVI. The last, on the eve of the Revolution, was to be Louis de Montmorency-Laval, Bishop of Metz and Chaplain to the king. For the Mont, ruled by the congregation of Saint Maur,* this was a period of declin by 1789 a mere dozen mon. watched over an abbey which had become too big and a virtually empty prison.* AG

The Grand-Rue,
*c.*1905.

■ COMMERCE
The other face of pilgrimage

Trade and commerce, which now flourish on a scale which may surprise visitors in search of tranquillity and contemplation, have always existed on the Mont. Shops are an inseparable and necessary part of pilgrimages,* if only to remind the traveller of the worldly life he must pass through on the path to the Almighty. The hum of business stops at the entrance to the abbey however.

The village* has its origins in such commerce in the Middle Ages,* when its inhabitants sold pilgrims' badges, made candles and ran hostels. When they visited the Mont, kings (see Royal Visits) very often also granted fiscal concessions to the villagers. Paradoxically it was the prison* which, in the nineteenth century, turned the village into an autonomous town clustered around its main street, known as the Grand-Rue. AG

■ Community

Benedictine* monks* led the monastic life on the Mont continuously from 966 to 1790. After being used as a prison* the abbey reverted briefly to its spiritual function between 1865 and 1886, when it received a group of diocesan missionaries summoned by Mgr Bravard, Bishop of Coutances and Avranches. Subsequently, it was not until 1969 that a religious community was established here once more. Following the precepts of Saint Benedict's Rule, this small community makes a point of welcoming all who wish to share its life of prayer and silence, and enjoys a considerable reputation. HD

Congregation of Saint Maur

An intellectual offshoot of the Benedictine* order, the Congregation of Saint Maur brought a genuine renewal of spiritual life to Mont-Saint-Michel when it became established there in 1622, at the height of the period of the commendatary abbots.* Throughout France the Maurists were distinguished as historians, and a great many medieval documents have survived thanks to their cataloguing and research work. Using the abbey archives as their primary source, Dom Jean Huynes and Dom Thomas Le Roy thus wrote a history of the Mont.

The abbey of the seventeenth and eighteenth centuries must be imagined complete with pictures and furniture and decorated in contemporary taste, as shown in the model* in the Invalides. It was at this time that the Maurist monks built the present western facade of the abbey church* – precursor in granite of European neo-classicism. A parvis was laid out in front of the church for processions. Gothic* austerity was abandoned in favour of this decorative style, common to all abbeys during the classical period, which itself was not destined to survive the shock of the Revolution, nor the 'medievalizing' restoration work of the nineteenth century. AC

■ CONSTRUCTION
Attracting crowds of master craftsmen

The great building projects of the Middle Ages* came into being with the Romanesque* style. In order to give concrete form to their innovatory ideas, the architect-monks required the services of highly skilled craftsmen, initially brought from Lombardy and elsewhere and later replaced by local masons.

On the Mont the architect Abbot Hildebert, inspired by the audacity and flair of Guillaume de Volpiano, conceived and built a

Figure of Geometry taken from a treatise on astronomy (detail), twelfth century. Avranches, Bibliothèque Municipale (ms 235, fol 33 recto).

'palace for the Archangel'. Granite ferried across from the Isles of Chausey* was hauled up the rock and dressed by stone cutters. Masons assembled the blocks and sealed them with mortar. Carpenters, roofers and a host of other skilled workers meanwhile swarmed over the scaffolding, surrounded by ladders, wooden cranes and wheel*-driven lifting gear.

During the Gothic* period similar building methods were employed, but architects were now lay specialists and the skills of stone cutters had greatly increased, while growing technical mastery allowed for increasing boldness in design. The first phase of reconstruction of the Flamboyant Gothic chancel* at Mont-Saint-Michel was quickly finished as the stones had all been cut and dressed in the quarries at Chausey.

Qualified workmen were paid a wage, and their masons' marks are still visible. Some tasks were carried out free of charge, some were paid, and some were exacted as feudal dues. GG

■ Conventional Buildings

At the head of each monastery Saint Benedict placed an abbot, from the the Syriac word meaning 'father', which has given us the word 'abbey'. Elected for life by the monks,* the abbot was the cornerstone of Benedictine* monasticism, with a duty to govern as a father – firmly but mercifully.

The buildings of a Benedictine abbey were designed to allow the monks to lead a life which can be summed up in the simple motto 'prayer and work'. First in importance was the abbey church,* where the community celebrated mass, vigils and the seven daily offices. Next to it lay the cloister.* Entirely closed to the outside world and opening only onto an interior garden, this covered passageway symbolized the monastic life. Surrounding it were the rooms in which the monks carried out their principal tasks – the chapter house,* refectory,* scriptorium* and dormitory.* Near by lay the various workshops and the farm which enabled the monastery to be self-sufficient. As hospitality (see Guest Chamber) was a duty imposed by the monastic rule, abbeys also had a guest house at a distance from the conventual buildings (see Almonry). On Mont-Saint-Michel the steep and rocky site made the usual layout impracticable: the various rooms had to be arranged one above the other rather than spread out around the cloister. Rooms for lodging pilgrims lay in the same building as those housing the monks, and the farm buildings were clustered around the priories.*

HD

View over the cloister and the upper level of the Merveille.

Corroyer (Edouard)

See Architects

Couesnon (River)

Canalized only in 1863, the River Couesnon no longer meanders at will. The vagaries of this river, which formed the border between Normandy* and Brittany,* made the precise extent of the two duchies a subject of controversy for many years. At the Revolution the matter was finally settled when the *départements* were laid out, and the boundary between Manche and Ille-et-Vilaine was drawn a little to the west. An old Breton saying still heard today is calculated to pique Norman pride: 'The Couesnon, in its folly, gave the Mont to Normandy.' AG

Crypts

The eleventh-century abbey church* on the Mont-Saint-Michel was built – like all sanctuaries dedicated to Saint Michael* – at the summit of the rock. As the upper level was not sufficiently wide to build on, the architect extended it by constructing three crypts: first that which was to support the chancel, then those of Saint Martin and Notre-Dame-des-Trente-Cierges, intended as foundations for the south and north arms of the transept respectively. For the remainder of the nave he simply modified Notre-Dame-sous-Terre.*

The Crypt of Saint Martin [33], dating from the years 1030-40, is built in a very simple style. Its semicircular barrel vault, spanning an impressive nine metres, is reinforced by a powerful transverse arch. A semidomed apse is let into the east end, while the soft light which penetrates the small windows let into the thickness of the walls is sufficient to emphasize the majestic sweep of the Romanesque* arches.

The River Couesnon with its barrage in the distance.

The Crypt of Notre-Dame-des-Trente-Cierges [38] presented a similar appearance before being altered in the thirteenth century, when the Merveille* was built. Some traces of the original painted decoration have survived. The statue of the Virgin Mary, dating from the thirteenth century, comes from the abbey of Hambye (Manche).

The chancel, under construction from 1023 and which collapsed in 1421, during the Hundred Years War,* was also built over a crypt, now incorporated into the stonework of the Crypte des Gros Piliers [42] which replaced it in the mid-fifteenth century. The discovery in 1964 of traces of this Romanesque crypt confirmed that the Romanesque chancel possessed an ambulatory – a common feature of pilgrimage* churches – three metres higher than the level of the nave.

The massive pillars of the Crypte des Gros Piliers, each five metres in circumference, support those of the chancel,* crowned thirty metres above by the pinnacles of the chevet. The prism-shaped ribs of the vaulting do not terminate in capitals, but rather flow directly into the walls and pillars themselves, with a precision that reveals the extent to which the stonemasons had succeeded in mastering the art of vaulting. HD

The Crypt of Saint Martin.

Overleaf:
The Crypte des Gros Piliers.

The Devil's
Dungeon.

37 Devil's Dungeon

The Devil's Dungeon* is a small thirteenth-century room which supports the small courtyard lying between the abbey church* and the cloisters.* The intersecting ribs of its vaulting* meet at a central pillar with a capital elegantly carved with foliage in low relief.

To the east, the room communicates with the crypt* known as Notre-Dame-des-Trente-Cierges via a single staircase reached through a twelfth-century archway. Along with its neighbour, which was redesigned in the thirteenth century, this is all that remains of the Romanesque building replaced by the Merveille.* During the nineteenth century, when the abbey became a prison,* this room was closed up and used to incarcerate recalcitrant prisoners. HD

50 Dormitory

In Benedictine* monasteries the monks' dormitory always lay very close to the church. Saint Benedict practised and recommended the constant praise of God. Consequently the monks would wake at night and make their way to the nearby church to sing to the glory of God. On the Mont, the Romanesque 'dorter' lies along the north side of the nave, at the same level. To make this possible two lower levels had first to be built, the Aquilon Chamber* and the Promenoir des Moines,* or

The dormitory seen from the West Terrace.

Du Guesclin (Bertrand)

The adventures of this younger son from Brittany* have passed into legend.* The man who rose to become Constable of France, covering himself with glory as well as with battle scars, was finally laid to rest in Saint Denis, the traditional burial place of the French sovereigns.

On the Mont-Saint-Michel can be seen the house which belonged to Tiphaine de Raguenel, wife of Bertrand Du Guesclin (*c.*1320-80).It is probable that Du Guesclin, governor of Pontorson in 1357, came to the Mont himself, and he installed his wife here in 1365, before leading an expedition of troublesome mercenaries to Spain in order to rid France of them. No more was needed for the Mont – a bastion of royalist patriotism – to adopt the figure of its most loyal defender. AG

Monks' Gallery. Connected with the church and cloister,* the dormitory also communicated with an infirmary* and the latrines.

The model* of 1701 shows its proportions before it was shortened, along with the western end of the nave, in the eighteenth century, by which time it no longer served its original purpose. Until the time of Robert de Torigni,* the abbot slept in the same room as his monks.* In the early days, it was his responsibility to wake them by ringing a bell. GG

Prose Chronicle of Bertrand Du Guesclin: Du Guesclin kneeling before Charles V (detail). Fifteenth century. Rouen, Bibliothèque Municipale (ms 1143, fol 4).

Anon. *Guillaume d'Estouteville,* early nineteenth century.
Oil on canvas.
72.5 × 63.5cm.
Rouen, Archevêché.

27 Dungeons

From the time of Robert de Torigni* the Mont possessed its own dungeons. Of these, two windowless cells known as the 'Twins' survive, in the coldest and dampest part of the buildings on the same level as the Aquilon.* Under Louis XIV the Mont became a state prison* to which detainees were consigned by warrant. Families who requested the arrest of a delinquent son often undertook to pay for the prisoner's confinement.

The community lived off the revenue thus generated. The former abbey lodgings* were transformed into a block of about forty cells, called the 'Great Exile', to which were brought prisoners such as Avedick, patriarch of Armenia, abducted from the island of Chios in 1706; the pamphleteer Dubourg, seized in Frankfurt in 1745; and a good number of clergy, madmen and political detainees. In 1786, the Comte de Vergennes, one of Louis XVI's ministers, wrote to the prior urging him to exercise 'humanity and wisdom' in his treatment of the prisoners. AG

Earth Tremors

The area around the Mont-Saint-Michel is not noted for its seismic activity, but a number of earth tremors have nevertheless been recorded there. In April 1155, according to the historian Dom Thomas Le Roy in 1647, 'there was such a great shaking of the ground at the Mont that all believed they should soon be buried. For this rock, the Mont de Tombe, which seems so firm and solid, did tremble at each shock as a leaf on a tree.' Other tremors occurred in November 1584, on 10 May 1619, and on 6 July 1640.

These tremors do not seem to have claimed any human casualties or caused material damage. More recently, on 6 December 1895, and 9 January and 16 November 1930, further slight earth tremors were registered. HD

Estouteville (Guillaume d')

Guillaume d'Estouteville (*c.*1403-83) was commendatary abbot* of the Mont from 1444 to 1482. His brother, Louis d'Estouteville, had successfully defended the Mont against all enemy assaults.

On his arrival, the new abbot undertook the reconstruction of the recently collapsed chancel,* quickly completed. Away from the Mont, his activities embraced the abbey church of Saint-Ouen in Rouen, where he was cardinal archbishop, and the church of Saint-Séverin in Paris, of which he was archpriest. These three buildings share architectural characteristics not found in any other examples of Flamboyant Gothic:* the absolute supremacy of the vertical, rising without interruption from floor level to the top of the vaulting; and the reduction and simplification of the wealth of decoration found in such profusion in other buildings of the fifteenth century. This exceptionally pure interpretation of Flamboyant Gothic, known as the 'Estouteville style', is characterized by its solidity, rigour, energy and vitality. As well as building churches at Gaillon, Rome, and Ostia of which he was bishop, the indefatigable cardinal was also a member of the king's council, a papal legate, a reformer of the university of Paris, and an active contributor to the revision of the trial of Joan of Arc. GG

Opposite:
View of the dungeons near the Aquilon Chamber, *c.*1910.

19 Fanils

The 'Chemin des Fanils' leads up to the conventual buildings* of the abbey, passing in front of the Gabriel Tower* and avoiding the Grand-Rue, or main thoroughfare. The building itself, which opens on to a gate leading down to the shore, dates only from 1828. Earlier buildings on this site have been used to store forage for horses and grain for the abbey.

The present 'Maison des Fanils', an imposing granite construction reminiscent of the barracks at Granville, was used as living quarters by the prison* guards during the nineteenth century. AG

View of the Fanils
and the Gabriel
Tower.

■ FAUNA AND FLORA
Seagulls and salicornia

Before the coming of the prison,* followed by tourism,* farming and fishing provided most of the livelihood of the Mont and its bay. Of the great variety of sea creatures to be found here – including the occasional dolphin offshore in summer and penguins in November – hake, mullet, shrimps and scallops are of principal interest to fishermen. Fish traps consisting of large wicker baskets called *bourraches* yield their catch at low tide, while fishermen and tourists try their luck with shrimping and fishing nets.

Small fish provide food for the many seabirds to be seen on the Mont, chiefly seagulls – for which Tombelaine* serves as a natural reserve – black-headed gulls, and grey plovers with their changing plumage.

On meadows submerged by the sea at high tide graze the prized *prés-salés* sheep. Their slightly salted meat is sometimes served with salicornia, or saltwort, which thrives on the nearby mudflats and is known by people living on the banks of the Couesnon* by the charming name of *haricot de mer.* AG

Féval (Paul)

The Breton novelist Paul Féval (1817-87) is remembered as the author of *Le Bossu (The Hunchback)*, a cloak-and-dagger tale of the adventures of the impetuous Lagardère.

Greatly attached to the region, he collected in *Les Merveilles du Mont-Saint-Michel* all the most celebrated legends* surrounding the Mont, and traced the history of its resistance during the Hundred Years War.* With *La Fée des Grèves (The Fairy of the Strand)*, published in 1850, he embarked upon a series of popular historical novels set in the bay,* followed by *A la plus Belle (To The Fairest)* and *L'Homme de Fer (The Iron Man)*. These epic romances of mysterious knights, heavily influenced by Sir Walter Scott, also feature kidnapped children, voracious peasants, and the enigmatic white-clad fairy to be seen wandering at dusk on the dunes near Saint-Méloir-des-Ondes. AG

Paul Féval
(1817-87).

'To crown it all, at the apex of the pyramid, where once the colossal gilded statue of the Archangel gleamed in splendour, are now four black sticks waving about: the telegraph. The wretched frettings of the affairs of this world on a spot once touched by thoughts of heaven! What a sorry sight.'

Victor Hugo, 1836.

Sheep grazing on the *prés salés* in the bay of Mont-Saint-Michel.

■ Fires

If three of the elements – earth, water and air – are essential components of the landscape of the Mont, the fourth – fire – has never been far away. The rock has always attracted not only lightning but also war and destruction, without which it would not have undergone the incessant process of rebuilding which has permitted each period to leave its architectural stamp. The complex history of the abbey runs hand in hand with tales of collapse and fire.

As early as 992 the abbey was consumed by flames, the start of a catalogue of disasters of one sort or another, including the collapse of part of the Romanesque nave in 1103 (see Abbey Church) and another fire in 1112.

In 1138 the people of the neighbouring town of Avranches put it to the torch during an uprising, and in 1204 it was the turn of the Breton Guy de Thouars. 1421 saw the ruin of the Romanesque chancel and 1433 yet another fire, while in 1594 lightning brought down the belltower. In 1776, after the twelfth serious fire, the first three bays of the nave of the abbey church were demolished. In 1834, finally, the prison* burned down. AG

1 Forward Gate

In about 1525, in order to fortify the entrance to the village,* the lieutenant Gabriel du Puy added a new forward gate beyond the Boulevard, known as the Avancée. It consisted of a triangular courtyard whose surrounding wall was pierced with a large opening for carts and another smaller one for pedestrians, similar to those of the

The Bourgeois Guardroom, courtyard and gateway of the Avancée.

King's Gate* and the Boulevard. The large gateway was secured by a swing door made from a panel which pivoted on a beam mounted horizontally across the entrance.

The Avancée was flanked by the Bourgeois Guardroom, which served as a shelter for the watchmen recruited from among the inhabitants of the village. Today it is the tourist information office.

Invaders who successfully penetrated this first gateway were faced with a crenellated terrace set against the rock face, from which defenders could easily repel them with musket fire. Two large cannon captured from the English by defenders of the Mont in 1434 are preserved in the courtyard of the Avancée. HD

Frémiet (Emmanuel)

A nephew and pupil of François Rude (1784-1855), the sculptor Frémiet (1824-1910) was at the peak of his career in Paris when the Third Republic – anticlerical and secular – commissioned him to design a monumental statue to top the neo-Gothic steeple* of the Mont-Saint-Michel.

First Frémiet made a small bronze model which could be taken apart (Dijon, Musée des Beaux-Arts). Like Viollet-le-Duc,* he imagined a gilded figure wielding a sword, faithful to the traditional symbolism associated with Saint Michael.* The statue met with instant success and was quickly adopted as the emblem of the Mont.

Following his usual practice, Frémiet exploited his work commercially, reproducing it as a trinket in different sizes. The badly eroded Archangel of the Mont was restored in 1987. AG

18 Gabriel (Tower)

Constructed in 1524 by the king's lieutenant Gabriel du Puy, the tower which bears his name was intended to defend the western slopes of the Mont and the Fanils.*

A large circular bastion sixteen metres across, it has walls from four and a half to three metres in thickness, sloping outwards at the base. Within, three superimposed banks of fortified gun emplacements surround a column set slightly off-centre to allow the gunners maximum room for manoeuvre. Hollow inside, the column acted as a flue to draw off the smoke from cannon fire. Wide embrasures in the form of horizontal slits, sharply splayed on the inside, allowed the cannon a broad field of fire.

The tower is crowned by a parapet resting on corbelled machicolations and set at a receding angle to deflect enemy

Emmanuel Frémiet, *Saint Michael the Archangel slaying the Dragon*. Statue of gilt bronze, restored and reinstated in 1987.

The Gabriel
Tower.

missiles. To reduce the risk of fire,* the construction is covered by a platform rather than the usual roofing timbers.

In 1627 the monks set up a windmill on this platform. HD

◼ Geology of the site

The bay* of Mont-Saint-Michel is a schistose depression of almost five hundred square kilometres opening into the Channel, into which flow three small coastal rivers: the Sée, Sélune and Couesnon.* It is overlooked by a number of granite outcrops, eighty to ninety metres high – at Carolles to the north, Avranches to the east, Saint-Broladre to the south, and Saint-Malo to the west.

In the middle of this flat expanse rise the islets of Mont-Dol,* Mont-Saint-Michel and Tombelaine,* outcrops of granulite, an extremely hard crys-

'We have been settled here on the Mont-Saint-Michel since yesterday morning. It is as frightfully cold and windy as in the month of March. Despite all that – Vive le Mont-Saint-Michel! No place could be more beautiful or savage, nowhere more grandiose or melancholy.'

Viollet-le-Duc, 1835.

talline rock. They emerged more than twenty million years ago, piercing the much softer schist above, which then hardened in contact with the granulite. The perimeter of the Mont at its base measures 950 metres, while its tip is eighty metres above sea level. HD

Opposite: Abbey church, view of flying buttresses of the chevet.

■ GOTHIC ARCHITECTURE
'God is Light'

The style of architecture known as Gothic was born in the mid-twelfth century in the Ile-de-France, a region in the forefront of a period of change and discovery for medieval society as a whole, and of an expansion in Christian awareness. The time was ripe for the flowering of cathedral architecture.

The development to become known as Gothic grew out of a combination of the eternal desire for light and the accumulated achievements of Romanesque* architecture: the need for light could now be satisfied thanks to the skill of the monk builders. At Saint-Denis in 1146 the architect and Benedictine Abbot Suger became one of the pioneers of this movement: having decided to rebuild the basilica, he sought to do away with the characteristic gloom of the Romanesque by replacing its cause – thick load-bearing walls – with huge stained glass windows.

As a result, other means had to be found to ensure the building's stability. The solution was to lie in the invention of a new structural framework: a large skeleton of slender stone members, fitted together so as to produce a stable and self-supporting framework. The skeleton of the new Gothic cathedrals was thus composed of rib vaulting* resting on internal pillars, supported by external piers and flying buttresses. This framework absorbed all the weight, thrusts and pressures generated by these tremendous buildings, channelling and balancing them until finally they disappeared to nothing. The outcome of this extraordinary defiance of gravity was a perfect equilibrium and stability. All that remained was to add the stained glass windows.

'God is Light': the theology of light was now and for centuries to come to govern sacred architecture throughout Europe. At the Mont, Robert de Torigni* lost no time in applying the new method of building, most notably to his now-vanished guest house.

The new architecture spread rapidly, feeling its way during the fifteenth century towards a more ornate style – Flamboyant Gothic – of which the chancel at the Mont is one of the finest surviving examples.

The term 'Gothic' was unknown in the Middle Ages, when the style was dubbed simply *'l'art français'*. It was left to the Renaissance to invent the name – as a term of disparagement. GG

21 Gouffre (Staircase)

See Châtelet

Gout (Paul)

See Architects

23 Grand Degré

The Grand Degré, or Great Stairway, leads up from the top of the Grand-Rue or main thoroughfare to give access to the abbey. Of its two parts the first, which lies outside the monastery, starts beyond the last village* houses and finishes at the Châtelet* and the stairway known as the 'Gouffre'. Its fine straight sweep is protected by a covered way which overhangs it, and by a barbican at the point where it joins the Châtelet. Inside the abbey, the great stair leads up from the guardroom* to the Terrasse du Saut-Gaultier,* from which the church is reached. This was the most perilous part of the ascent for any potential assailants, who would come under fire from defenders overhead while being pinned to the spot by a fortified bridge and portcullis. During the Hundred Years War* the principle of extending an open welcome to pilgrims* was to find its counterpart in an equally stringent system of defence. GG

22 Guardroom

The guardroom lies on the ground floor of the building erected by Abbot Richard Turstin in the mid-thirteenth century against the apse of the abbey church,* in order to protect the new ecclesiastical courtroom, later to be known as the Belle-Chaise,* on the level above. It also served as a gatehouse, the main entrance to the monastery having been moved to this spot near the almonry* and Merveille* in the thirteenth century. In the fifteenth century, when the Mont became a fortress, it was turned into a guardroom, where guests other than princes of the blood were required to leave their weapons before entering the monastery.

The floor follows the slope of the rock, rising in steps which divide the room into three bays, with elegant rib vaulting* of decreasing height; the highest bay was lowered in the fifteenth century, when the chancel* of the abbey church was built. At the end of the fourteenth century, a handsome fireplace was added opposite the main doorway. From this room the church can be reached via the Grand Degré.* HD

Opposite:
The Grand Degré leading up to the abbey.

Emile Sagot,
The Guardroom.
Watercoloured drawing.
Musée d'Avranches.

40 GUEST CHAMBER

The Guest Chamber, one of the Merveille's* three dining halls which lie one above the other, is situated between the almonry* on the ground floor and the monks' refectory.* It was used for the reception of distinguished guests who had come on pilgrimage,* and also served as a dormitory.

Divided down the centre by a row of tall, slender columns, it is generously lit throughout by high, narrow windows. At the far western end was a huge double fireplace, which served as a kitchen and could be closed off by a tapestry when the remainder of the hall was in use. An entrance porch, the Magdalene chapel [41] and latrines concealed in the wall completed the ensemble.

This magnificent reception room lost much of its splendour when the original polychrome decor disappeared – as it has in most great medieval buildings. The original colours must be imagined in their dazzling heyday, when the columns, vaulting and walls would all have been painted, while the floor was covered with glazed tiles in red and green picked out with thousands of gilded fleurs-de-lis and Castilian towers. This enchanting space would be bathed in sunlight streaming in through the stained glass windows.

When feasts were held here two tables covered with white cloths were set out lengthways in the aisles, the one on the south side being presided over by the abbot, who sat with his back to the central fireplace.

Saint Benedict had stipulated that 'each guest should be given the honour due to him'. Thus if the guest happened to be a prince or king, the hospitality was accordingly regal, in an architectural setting designed to be of the utmost elegance, refinement and luxury. Of the lavish ceremonies staged here to accompany royal visits,* some – notably those in honour of François I – have gone down in history. GG

■ Historic Monument

During an inspection tour of Basse-Normandie in 1841, Prosper Mérimée – inspector of historic monuments since 1834 – noted on visiting Mont-Saint-Michel that the nave and transept of the abbey church* were in a deplorable condition.

The abbey was used at this period as a prison,* and the chaplain, Abbé Lecourt, requested funds in order to undertake restoration work. In a letter to Ludovic Vitet, Mérimée did not hide his scepticism: 'Abbé Lecourt would like us to give money to restore his nave, but if it were restored they would promptly install more prison cells in it and our money would be wasted. It is not up to us to provide lodgings for Monsieur Barbès et al.'

Mérimée remained otherwise unmoved by the abbey. In the same letter he remarks of the chancel: 'I used to harbour some vague admiration for the Gothic architecture of the Mont-Saint-Michel. On this occasion it struck me as dreadful. Granite is most unsuitable for pinnacles and croziers ... and the salty mists of the west have already finished off all the mouldings, which look like lumps of sugar soaked in water.'

It is not difficult to deduce from this why it took so long for the abbey to be listed as a historic monument. Indeed it was not until 1874, two years after the appointment of Edouard Corroyer as architect* in charge of restoration, that it was taken over by the Service for Historic Monuments. The ramparts* were finally listed only in 1908. HD

■ HUNDRED YEARS WAR
The Mont remains French

In 1346 Edward III of England, who had laid claim to the throne of France, landed on the coast of the Cotentin peninsula, thus starting a war which was to continue for over a century, until 1450. As the conflict grew, the abbot of Mont-Saint-Michel became responsible for the defence of the island. In 1357 he became titular captain of the garrison, a function which he delegated to a military commander – thus bringing Bertrand Du Guesclin* to the Mont as its captain. The war, which had been fought sporadically during the fourteenth century, escalated in intensity in the fifteenth. By 1419 the whole of Normandy* was under English occupation, with the sole exception of the Mont. Even the small island of Tombelaine* was overrun, but the Mont had a natural defence in the sea, which cut it off more frequently than it does today (see Tides), as well as being ringed by powerful ramparts,* planned by Abbot Jolivet* and improved upon by the captain of the garrison Louis d'Estouteville. It also received assistance from the people of Saint-Malo, and was defended by 119 Norman knights. Consequently, in spite of the defection of Jolivet in 1420 and the collapse of the chancel* of the abbey church in 1421, it succeeded in remaining French. HD

Cannon in the court of the Avancée (Forward Gate).

51 Infirmary

In order to avoid the spread of infection among healthy monks by the sick, who were also allowed a less restricted diet, monasteries always had an infirmary. Over the centuries the infirmary on the Mont has been in a number of different places. The first infirmary was a small Romanesque room on the northern side of the dormitory* with which it communicated, the floor of the infirmary lying lower than that of the dormitory, which was raised in the twelfth century.

Robert de Torigni* laid out a new infirmary above the lodgings which he built to the south [25]. More accessible, it also had the practical advantage of direct communication with the chapel of Saint-Etienne,* which served as a mortuary. In the

Previous pages: Restoration of the cloister by the Historic Monuments, c.1880.

late fourteenth century, Abbot Pierre Le Roy transferred the infirmary to the abbey lodgings;* it was his intention to put it between Belle-Chaise* and the Merveille,* but the planned building was never erected. HD

■ Iron Cage

Both legend and literature have adopted the so-called 'daughters' of Louis XI, in which prisoners were suspended from the ceiling and driven mad. Their supposed inventor, Cardinal La Balue, is reputed to have been one of their first victims at Loches (Indre-et-Loire). One of these cages, reconstructed using fifteenth-century carpentry and ironworking techniques, can now be seen in the keep there.

An iron cage was still in use at the Mont-Saint-Michel in the reign of François I. In the seventeenth century, the Benedictine* François de Chavigny spent thirteen years incarcerated in it. Under Louis XVI, the cage, by that time no longer in use, was destroyed as a relic of a barbarous age. It remains the most potent symbol of the time when the Mont was a prison, and when the monks themselves were responsible not only for guarding the prisoners but also for their punishment (see Dungeons). AG

'The devastation is barbaric. Imagine a prison – hat is this indescribably hideous and fetid thing which they call a prison – installed within the magnificent surroundings of priests and fourteenth-century knights. It is a toad in a reliquary.'

Victor Hugo, 1836.

The Iron Cage of Mont-Saint-Michel. Engraving from *Prisons on Mont-Saint-Michel from 1425 to 1864* by Etienne Dupont.

■ ISLAND CHARACTER OF THE MONT
Threats and counter-measures

The insularity of Mont-Saint-Michel, which has always been a major element in its fascination, is today under threat. The long history of the site is a romance in itself. Ten thousand years before our era, global warming raised the level of the sea, then a hundred metres below today's level. At that time, the future Mont-Saint-Michel was still part of the mainland. From 7000 to 5500BC, sea level rose from forty metres below its current level to within ten. Meanwhile the encroaching sea formed the Channel, and by about 4000BC it was within three metres of the present-day shoreline: the Mont was cut off from the mainland.

-10 000

-7 000 à -5 500

-4 000

From the start the island was threatened with silting,* initially from natural causes, then increasingly from human intervention, notably the creation of polders* in the nineteenth century. The vexed question of how to restore the rock's isolation has prompted a number of proposed conservation measures. Some have suggested total or partial removal of the causeway,* others favour replacing it with a route on piles or a raised walkway. But however elegant or sophisticated these solutions may be, none can halt the advancing sands.

Alternative schemes, on the other hand, envisage stopping or even reversing the process of silting. Their method is simple: to restore and even increase the former process by which the rivers which flowed into the bay also scoured the shore. The flattening of the dyke at Roche-Torin in 1983 was the first step on the way to setting this natural hydraulic system back in motion. This, in combination with the appreciable rise in sea level forecast for the twenty-first century, gives hope that the Mont in its unique setting, designated by UNESCO* as a world heritage site, will indeed remain an island. GG

Jolivet (Robert)

In the gallery of abbots of Mont-Saint-Michel, Robert de Torigni,* the great abbot of the golden age, finds his opposite extreme in the reviled figure of Robert Jolivet (died 1444), the treacherous abbot who laid down his arms to the Duke of Bedford, brother of Henry V, thus siding with the English at the height of the Hundred Years War.* Yet it was Jolivet who had overseen the construction of defences on the rock in the years following Agincourt in 1415, when the whole of Normandy* was under English occupation with the sole exception of the Mont. He even had a cistern* built and modernized the ramparts,* only to lay siege to his own fortifications, fighting alongside the English in 1425. Although notions of treason and betrayal are perhaps inappropriate in the context of the period – in previous centuries the Mont had after all received the protection of the English king, who was also Duke of Normandy* – the abbot's defection, preceded by the collapse of the Romanesque* chancel,* nevertheless rendered the defence of the Mont in those troubled times all the more heroic. AG

3 King's Gate and Tower

The entrance to the village* between the Tour du Roi (King's Tower) and the Tour de l'Arcade was almost certainly built by Abbot Jolivet.* Around 1435, Captain Louis d'Estouteville had a more heavily fortified gateway erected, called the 'King's Gate' because it also housed the officer responsible for guarding it on behalf of the French king. Flanked to the south by the King's Tower, the gate is still equipped with a portcullis and is preceded by a moat over which a drawbridge – rebuilt in 1992 – can be lowered. There is an external carriage gateway and a postern gate for pedestrians, but only one entrance on the side which opens on to the village street.

To reinforce the King's Gate, in 1445 Louis d'Estouteville had a projecting bastion constructed in front of it, known as the Boulevard, with a wall pierced alternately with loopholes for archers and embrasures for cannon. The double entrance of the Boulevard, consisting of carriage-gate and postern, is in turn flanked by a semicircular tower set against the solid rock. A second barbican – the Forward Gate* or Avancée – was added later, completing an already highly sophisticated defence system. HD

Arms of Robert Jolivet on the rampart walls.

Opposite: Richard Parkes Bonington (1801-28), *The Mont-Saint-Michel* (detail). Watercolour and gouache on paper. Calais, Musée des Beaux-Arts.

Above right: Georges Bouet, *The King's Gate and Tower.* Engraving from *The History and Description of Mont-Saint-Michel* by Edouard Le Héricher, Caen, 1848.

39 KNIGHTS' CHAMBER

Built over the storeroom,* the Knights' Chamber supports the cloister* above (see Merveille), and formed part of the enclosure of the Gothic* monastery. It was not originally known by its present name, being used as a scriptorium in the Middle Ages. Its size and beauty are no doubt due to the intellectual prestige of the Romanesque monastic foundation under Robert de Torigni.* This new temple of the written word would have housed large cabinets, numerous reading desks and an area set aside for the copying of manu-scripts.* It was conceived on a grand scale in order to host the celebrated congresses of scholars which pre-ceded the founding of the universi-ties in the thirteenth century.

The place of study had also to be a place of light – in keeping with the Gothic spirit and in order to serve the practical needs of reading and copy-ing of manuscripts. With its clear glass windows and broad, north-facing façade, it was an ideal studio for the work of illuminators. As the copying of manuscripts began to die out, however, the room was used

simply as a library and perhaps as the chapter house.* In winter it served as the calefactory, or warming-room, on account of its two splendid fireplaces. At the western end a large opening, now glazed over, was intended to communicate with another building which was never constructed. Around the room are latrines concealed in the walls. The ground plan is considerably larger than that of the storeroom, but smaller than that of the cloister. The gradual increase in size of rooms built on successively higher levels was a stroke of genius on the part of the architect, allowing the cloister to open out into an almost complete square. An impressive forest of columns divides the room into four aisles. The shafts of the columns are robust, the sculpture of the capitals vigorous, and the intersecting ribs of the vaulting* strongly modelled. The architect has succeeded in creating here a distinct atmosphere of repose and strength, and an architecture well suited to the Benedictine virtues of solidity, patience and endurance. GG

55 Kitchens. See Refectory

■ Lace staircase

The lateral thrust imposed by ribbed vaulting* on the pillars which support it has a tendency to make buildings in the Gothic* style bulge outwards. Medieval master builders had the idea of re-directing these lateral forces by means of permanent supports – flying buttresses – into perpendicular abutments or piers of masonry, whose vertical force was increased by the weight of crowning pinnacles. The chancel* of the abbey church* on the Mont is supported by two tiers of flying buttresses, with piers surmounted by a thicket of pinnacles. The exuberance of the external decoration makes a

■ LEGENDS
Ancient miracles to modern myths

'When I was at the summit, I said to the monk who accompanied me: "Father, how good it must be to dwell here!" He replied: "Sir, it is a very windy place"; and so we began talking as we watched the incoming tide ... And the monk told me stories, all the ancient tales of the place, legends and more legends.' Maupassant, in *La Horla,* thus recalls the legacy of myth surrounding the Mont. The miracles* attributed to Saint Michael* – which attracted pilgrimages* in the Middle Ages* – should not be confused with legends about the foundation of the Mont, associated with the figure of Aubert.* The most celebrated of these tells how, a year after the appearance of the Archangel to the bishop, the immense forest of Scissy, which covered the entire bay,* was swept away by a tidal wave. The story, inspired perhaps by an historical event such as forest clearance, symbolizes redemption, the founding of a holy city after a purifying cataclysm. In legend the Mont is also related to the destruction of a town called 'Ys' – mirrored in the Breton legend of a town submerged in the 'Baie des Trépassés' off Douarnenez – the remains of which are said still to lie beneath the waters of the 'Mare de Bouillon'.

Legend lives on. As the pianist François Chaplin started to play Claude Debussy's prelude entitled *La Cathédrale engloutie* in the abbey church in 1994, it is said that the abbey bell could be heard ringing in sympathy. AG

sharp contrast with the sobriety of the interior.

The jewel of this complex is without doubt the Escalier de Dentelle, or Lace Staircase, so-named because of the delicate carving of its Flamboyant Gothic stonework, and reached by means of a spiral staircase built into one of the piers. As at the cathedral of Senlis, it spans one of the flying buttresses. From it there is a superb view of the chevet, the village* and the bay.* HD

■ Manuscripts

The books and manuscripts formerly belonging to the abbey were taken to Avranches in 1791 and placed in the Bibliothèque Municipale, where they constitute the most valu-

able part of the collection. Two hundred and three manuscripts from the Mont-Saint-Michel are preserved there, all but four of them dating back to the Middle Ages.

Many branches of knowledge are represented in the collection, testifying to the extensive culture of the monks:* apart from patristic and theological works, there are also works on philosophy, include thirty-one treatises by Aristotle, ancient classical texts by Cicero, Seneca and Pliny, and treatises on history, music and astronomy.

Manuscripts actually produced on the Mont date principally from the Romanesque period; the names of fourteen copyist monks have come down to us, including a certain Fromond who, not without a touch of vanity, inscribed a work of Saint Ambrose with the words: 'Happy Fromond. There is a monk who has earned eternal love!'

The scriptorium* reached the peak of its output between 1050 and 1080, when manuscripts were decorated with magnificent full-page illustrations and marvellous illuminated letters, peopled with human figures and animals against a background of interwoven tracery and foliage. It again became very prolific under the abbotcy of Robert de Torigni,* with generally less ornate manuscripts, with the exception of the cartulary of the abbey and a chronicle composed by the abbot himself. It went into decline during the thirteenth century: henceforth, manuscript works were to become the almost exclusive preserve of secular workshops set up in conjunction with the new universities. HD

Georges Bouet, *The Lace Staircase.* Engraving taken from *The History and Description of Mont-Saint-Michel,* by Edouard Le Héricher, Caen, 1848.

Cartulary of Mont-Saint-Michel: the Dream of Saint Aubert, mid-twelfth century. Avranches, Bibliothèque Municipale (ms 210, fol 4 verso).

Edouard Corroyer, *Projected general restoration: entrance to the abbey and buildings of the Merveille,* March 1879. Watercoloured drawing. Paris, Bibliothèque du Patrimoine.

■ MERVEILLE

Clinging to the north flank of the rock, the Gothic* monastery known as the Merveille, or Marvel, was built at the beginning of the thirteenth century. The restricted space available forced builders to move ever upwards, climbing towards the sky. On the eastern side were constructed, in ascending order, the almonry,* guest chamber,* and monks' refectory;* at the western end, the storeroom,* Knights' Chamber,* and cloister.* The whole complex, measuring eighty metres across, took seventeen years to build and was completed in 1228. This wonder of the art of construction was a remarkable challenge: a skyscraper fifty metres high, perched on a vertical cliff and subject to tremendous internal stresses from the lateral thrust of its vaults. On the central level, the guest and Knights' Chambers are lightened by a particularly skilful exercise in Gothic building techniques, most notably in the balancing of stresses from the vaulting, which is of a rare perfection. The minimum of support thus produces the maximum of space and light. But it is on the upper level of the refectory and cloister that the greatest ingenuity is displayed. The light that floods through the walls of the refectory is the result of a fine balance between structural solidity and the window spaces allowed. This cellular method of construction was seven centuries ahead of its time. In the cloister, meanwhile, the three-dimensional structure with its grouping of columns in threes, creates an architecture* of stability and lightness.

Over and above the technical skills of their builders, each chamber of the Merveille also served a specific function in the organization of the monastery. Visitors are frequently astonished by the difference in atmosphere between them. Three dining halls placed one above the other – the almonry, guest chamber and refectory, so different despite their similar size – are equally surprising too: security below, feasting in the middle, serenity above. From the outside the Merveille is grandiose, especially its impressive northern façade, supported by a series of buttresses each rising in a single vertical sweep of thirty metres. The spectacular quality of its architecture* is a major element in the fascination exercised by this palace of the Archangel. GG

■ MICHAEL (SAINT): A CULT FROM THE EAST

An interest in angels is a very ancient phenomenon and a feature common to many religions. In Christianity, both the Old and the New Testaments make frequent reference to them. According to Christian tradition, angels are superior spirits created by God, hosts of whom are permanently before him, adoring and singing his glory. The love they bear for him reaches out to the universe: in communicating it to men they are thus messengers from heaven.

In the Book of Revelation (12:7-8), Saint John wrote: 'And there was war in heaven. Michael and his angels fought against the dragon; and the dragon fought and his angels, and prevailed not; neither was their place found any more in heaven.' Mikaël is a Hebrew name which means 'who is like God?'; in other words, no one can equal God. Born in the east at the beginning of the fourth century, the cult of the Archangel reached Ireland, Italy – notably at Monte Gargano – and, through the ministrations of Bishop Aubert* in the eighth century, what was to become Normandy.* Michael's reputation as the definitive champion of good over the forces of evil and as benevolent dispenser of justice attracted crowds of devoted pilgrims* to his shrine. Medieval iconography focused on his twin tasks of salvation, portraying him armed with a lance or sword for combat, and a balance as the instrument of the last judgement. GG

Anon, *Saint Michael slaying the Dragon,* seventeenth century. Oil on canvas. Musée d'Avranches.

■ Middle Ages

The Middle Ages – the period between the great invasions (see Norman Invasions) and the beginning of the Renaissance – were also the age which saw the birth of western Europe.

The early period known as the Dark Ages lasted from the collapse of the ancient Roman Empire, in the fourth and fifth centuries, until the eleventh century. This was a time of great turmoil and upheaval, with the influence of barbarian invaders, the legacy of the ancient Roman and Celtic civilizations, and the development of the monastic movement all preparing the way for the flowering of a great new civilization. This was the background against which Mont-Saint-Michel was founded (in the eighth century), the church of Notre-Dame-sous-Terre* was built, and Normandy* was founded by the Vikings.

In the early eleventh century there emerged a new style of architecture later to be known as Romanesque.* On the Mont, this was to be the style adopted for the first abbey buildings. All the necessary conditions were now in place for the emergence of a new order: western societies now conformed to a strongly hierarchical structure in feudalism, and each of the developing provinces was governed by a feudal lord with a steadily increasing range of powers. By the period just before the first crusades, the celebrated Dukes of Normandy, and particularly William the Conqueror,* had succeeded in elevating their province to the level of the great European powers.

In 1204, Normandy became part of the kingdom of France. Prosperity grew, the influence of the cities and towns spread, and schools and universities were founded under the authority of the church.

The Gothic* style was now emerging: cathedrals flooded with light were springing up, as was the Merveille* on the Mont-Saint-Michel. A period of social stability, the thirteenth century was also a time of enlightenment; the influence of French art and ideas spread throughout Europe, with a vitality founded on a strong sense of communal purpose allied with the remarkable personalities of the men and women who were the chief protagonists of their era. During the fourteenth and fifteenth centuries, the synthesis of the medieval world fell apart, ushering in a time of crisis, prey to doubt, famine, plague and war.*

During the Renaissance and afterwards, the term 'medieval' was used to denote obscurantism, with pejorative connotations now lost. GG

■ Miracles

Centres of pilgrimage* have always tended to foster tales of miracles. At the Mont-Saint-Michel the earliest accounts of miracles were recorded in the eleventh century, encouraging pilgrims to make the journey to the sanctuary of the Archangel in ever greater numbers.

Some stories related the appearance of Saint Michael* himself in the guise of flames at night – often so bright that those who saw them, such as Bishop Norgod of Avranches, were convinced that the abbey was on fire. The majority of the tales concerned pilgrims who had come to venerate the relics, such as a Burgundian who with the abbot's permission took home with him a stone from the Mont to have it enshrined in the altar of a church dedicated to Saint Michael. After his death, his widow neglected the church, which fell into disrepair. On pilgrimage to Saint Michel, she was stopped in her tracks before the Mont by a supernatural force and only allowed to reach the abbey after promising to restore her own church.

Perhaps the most poignant story concerns a pregnant woman who found herself in labour while out on the sands. So passionately did she pray that the waters of the incoming tide* separated around her, allowing her to give birth safely in the midst of the waves. To commemorate this miracle the monks erected a great cross – la Croix des Grèves – which eventually vanished beneath the sands. HD

The Limbourg Brothers, *Les Très Riches Heures du Duc de Berry: le Mont-Saint-Michel, c.1390.* Chantilly, Musée Condé (ms 65, fol 195 recto).

Model of Mont-
Saint-Michel,
c.1701.
Paris, Musée des
Plans en relief,
Hôtel des
Invalides.

◼ Model

One of the masterpieces of the museum of models in the Hôtel National des Invalides in Paris is a scale model of the Mont-Saint-Michel made in 1701, a copy of which can be seen at the abbey. The Mont appears precisely as it was in Louis XIV's time: now vanished buildings re-emerge in remarkable detail; the nave of the abbey church* and the dormitory* are shown with their original dimensions; and one of the towers of the façade is still in place, as are the lodgings of Robert de Torigni.* The last Gothic steeple* had already disappeared by this time, to be replaced by a bulbous belfry. The gable ends of the nave and Merveille,* which can be opened on the Paris model, reveal the eighteenth-century interior decor. GG

◼ Monks

The words 'monk' and 'monastery' derive from the Greek word *monos,* meaning 'alone'. Monks withdraw from the world in order to please God alone. 'Anchorites' or 'hermits' led solitary lives, such as those who lived on Mont-Tombe* before the coming of Saint Aubert.* The great majority of monks, now as in the Middle Ages, are cenobites, living together as brothers in a community according to a rule. The most famous of these is the one drawn up by Saint Benedict at the beginning of the sixth century, requiring obedience, humility and silence. Benedictine* monks also take the vows of chastity, poverty and obedience common to all the Christian orders, as well as one of stability, by which they are attached to their abbey for life (see Conventual Buildings).

These were the Benedictine monks in whose hands the sanctuary of the Mont lay from 966 to 1790. In the heyday of the monastery, under Abbot Robert de Torigni,* there were sixty of them; by 1790 there were barely a dozen. HD

■ Mont-Dol

This granite outcrop, sixty-four metres high, is an ideal viewpoint from which to discover the western part of the bay.*

Men lived here as long ago as palaeolithic times, as was proved by a large deposit of prehistoric animal bones discovered here in 1872, and by the neolithic period the rock had undoubtedly become a place of worship. Roman legionaries founded a sanctuary to Mithras here, later to be replaced by Christians with a chapel in honour of Saint Michael.* In 1158, the Archbishop of Dol gave it to the monks of Mont-Saint-Michel, who turned it into a small priory,* traces of which can still be seen around the present nineteenth-century buildings.

Georges Bouet, *Monks in the Guest Chamber.* Engraving from *The History and Description of Mont-Saint-Michel* by Edouard Le Héricher, Caen, 1848.

A wealth of legends surrounds the rock. According to one of them, the Devil challenged the Archangel here, only to be vanquished with ease. On a rock near the church are marks said to be the Devil's claw marks, as well as a footprint left by the Archangel as he leapt in a single bound back to Mont-Saint-Michel! HD

◼ Mont-Tombe

Mont-Saint-Michel was originally called Mont-Tombe, from the low Latin *tumba,* signifying both 'tumulus' and 'tomb'. According to the historian Guillaume de Saint-Pair, a twelfth-century monk, pious hermits in the sixth century built two sanctuaries on the Mont-Tombe, one dedicated to Saint Etienne, and the other to the martyr of Autun, Saint Symphorien. These anchorites were provisioned by a priest from Astériac (Beauvoir), who brought over essential supplies on a donkey.

The original name of Tombelaine* was probably *tumbella* or 'little tomb', and accordingly the sanctuary built by Aubert* in 708 was known by chroniclers as the church of Saint Michael of the Tombs. The name Mont-Saint-Michel came into use at the beginning of the tenth century, probably when pilgrimages* started to become more frequent. HD

Abbey of Hambye (Manche).

◼ NORMAN ABBEYS
A spiritual and intellectual network

Since Merovigian times a network of abbeys had existed on Norman territory. William the Conqueror* was to strengthen it, and to lay the foundations of a similar circle of abbeys in England, including Saint Michael's Mount in Cornwall. The richest of the French foundations, the abbey of Bec, enjoyed especially close links with the Mont-Saint-Michel.

Today, a tour of the Norman abbeys is a good way of gaining a better understanding of the place held by the Mont-Saint-Michel in its own world: from Jumièges and Saint-Wandrille – distant sister houses – via the wealthy abbeys of Caen which contain the tombs of William and his wife Mathilda, to the closest, Hambye and La Lucerne d'Outremer, whose building doubtless owes some-

thing to the skill of architects from the Mont. The latter, a few kilometres from the bay,* is worth a special visit. Reduced to a romantic ruin during the Revolution and the nineteenth century, it has been completely rebuilt in recent years.

It is impossible to view the Mont-Saint-Michel in isolation from this community of fortified abbeys, with which it maintained not only spiritual but also economic links and scholarly exchanges – as is demonstrated by the circulation of manuscripts* between them. AG

Normandy

In 911, the treaty of Saint-Clair-sur-Epte conceded the duchy of Normandy to Rollo, who had converted to Christianity. The links which his dynasty subsequently forged with the Mont – a visible symbol of its prestige and power – went from strength to strength as time passed. A spiritual focal point of the duchy, which gradually established Norman power in England and Sicily, the Mont nevertheless remained predominantly a fortress, prized for its strategic position. In 1091 William the Conqueror's* son Henry I, King of England, resisted attacks on the Mont by his two brothers, Robert Curthose and William Rufus.

It was the duke's privilege to choose the abbot: thus Roger II, Prior of Jumièges, was sent to the Mont by Henry I. It was the political union of Abbot Robert de Torigni* and Henry II of England which made possible the most magnificent period in the history of the Mont.

Little by little, from being a Norman monument which only just escaped falling into English hands and had occasionally been saved by the Bretons, the Mont became, from the time of Joan of Arc and Louis XI (founder of the Order of Saint-Michel*), a monument belonging to the French nation as a whole. AG

Norman Invasions

At the time of the Viking raids, all the religious communities in the region which was to become Normandy* withdrew to more peaceful parts of the country, with the apparent exception of the canons installed by Saint Aubert* on the Mont-Tombe.* Evidence shows that pilgrims continued to pray here to Saint Michael* despite the ever present dangers from Viking pirates.

Not only was the Mont spared from the Vikings, but it had already forged links with the most important pilgrimage centres in Christendom. The conditions of relative peace enjoyed by the region were due largely to the protection of Brittany,* to whom Charles the Bald had ceded the Cotentin peninsula in 867. HD

Order of Saint-Michel

In 1210, it is believed, Philippe Auguste founded in Paris the 'Confraternity of Saint-Michel-l'Ange of the Mont in the sea'. When Louis XI instituted the Order of Saint-Michel at the château of Amboise in 1469, his motives were not merely pious. At a time when prowess on the battlefield had yielded to pragmatic diplomacy, it was

Cartulary of Mont-Saint-Michel: solemn donation of Richard II, Duke of Normandy, mid-twelfth century. Avranches, Bibliothèque Municipale (ms 210, fol 18).

Jean Fouquet, *Statutes of the Order of Saint-Michel: The King accompanied by the first fifteen Knights of the Order, 1470.* Paris, Bibliothèque nationale de France (ms Fr 19819, fol 1).

26 NOTRE-DAME-SOUS-TERRE

The most ancient surviving part of the abbey, this venerable church originally stood above ground on the western side of the summit of the Mont. In the eleventh century it was turned into foundations for the first three bays of the nave of the abbey church,* and was swallowed up by the Romanesque monastery which surrounded it to the north, west and south (see Crypts). Since the destruction of the first bays of the nave in 1776, it has lain beneath the west terrace.*

It is of modest proportions; ignoring the pseudo-narthex, added in the eleventh century and forming the entrance today, it makes an irregular quadrilateral about twelve metres long by nine metres wide.

The exact date of its construction is not known, but its masonry is characteristic of techniques in use before the year 1000, with very thick walls of crudely squared granite blocks placed sideways on, arches lined with flat tiles, and piers in which granite blocks alternate with courses of brick. It is possible that it was built during the first half of the tenth century by the successors of the canons installed by Saint Aubert,* or by the first Benedictine* monks* shortly after 966, as a result of the generosity of Richard I, Duke of Normandy.*

A central wall pierced by two rounded arches divides it into two parallel aisles, each ending in a sanctuary at the east end with a flat chevet covered by a gallery. This curious layout is doubtless due to subsequent alterations. Indeed it is possible that the central wall and niches forming the sanctuaries were added later in order to support a building above which has since disappeared – perhaps a pre-Romanesque abbey church, larger than Notre-Dame-sous-Terre, which was

taken down when the Romanesque nave of the abbey church was built. Restoration work on Notre-Dame-sous-Terre, started in 1960 by the architect* Yves-Marie Froidevaux, brought to light a wall of cyclopean masonry lying behind the right-hand sanctuary which might be the remains of the oratory built by Saint Aubert in 708. This church would then have replaced the primitive sanctuary, which thus became the modest kernel from which was to spring the monumental complex so admired today. HD

more essential than ever to invent ideals to preoccupy a newly pacified nobility. In the face of the powerful duchy of Burgundy under Charles the Bold, who conferred the Order of the Golden Fleece, the King of France, modelling himself on King Arthur, gathered round him a court of chivalry which included a select band of knights who were to be the earthly defenders of the Archangel.

The Order evolved in parallel with the monarchy: relegated to a less prestigious rank by the Order of the Holy Spirit, created by Henri III, it continued, with the military Order of Saint-Louis, to be one of the orders conferred by the king until the eighteenth century. Already by the time of Montaigne, who proudly wore its ribbon, membership of the Order of Saint-Michel was reserved mainly for men of letters. The black ribbon of Saint-Michel still worn under the Restoration in the nineteenth century no longer had any connection with the Archangel. AG

34 Ossuary

The abbey ossuary, or charnel-house, lay near the monks'* cemetery on the southern side of the rock, not far from the mortuary chapel, now the chapel of Saint Etienne.* Funeral rites were an occasion of great solemnity but also of hope, for the day of death in this world was considered the day of birth into the true life of the next. As the burial ground was small, like all medieval cemeteries, it had to be cleared from time to time. The bones were then arranged compactly in walled-up ossuaries.

The monks' ossuary lies next to the great wheel:* concealed by the walls, it would have passed unnoticed. In the Middle Ages,* the proximity of tombs and ossuaries was not considered morbid, but was accepted as a manifestation of the communion of saints. GG

The monks' ossuary near the great wheel.

Painters

Artists of the romantic period were well aware of the advantages of using medieval monuments as models for their work. At Mont-Saint-Michel they were unable to enter the abbey until after the prison* was closed down in 1863 (with the exception of Viollet-le-Duc, who had been recommended by Mérimée), and so were obliged to content themselves with depicting general views or details of the village* houses.

Among the painters who have worked here are a number of very celebrated artists, including Bonington, who executed a superb watercolour of the south side of the Mont; Corot who made drawings of the Porte du Roi (King's Gate) and the Maison de l'Arcade; Théodore Rousseau, who painted the village street and several picturesque houses; and Eugène Isabey, whose canvas, painted in 1840, shows the Mont menaced by the tumultuous seas and storm-laden skies so typical of his work.

Other nineteenth-century artists also made the Mont the subject of their work, including Félix Benoit, Georges Bouet, Eugène Cicéri, Hippolyte Lalaisse, Charles Séchan and Deroy. Conversely, neither Géricault, a native of Mortain, nor Millet, born in Gréville, nor Delacroix, who was a frequent visitor to Normandy,* seems to have evinced any interest in the Mont or its bay.* In the twentieth century, Paul Signac is alone among the great painters in depicting the Mont. HD

12 Parish Church

The statue of Joan of Arc, who was witness to the prestige of Saint Michael* during the Hun-

The parish church and cemetery.

dred Years War,* welcomes the visitor to the village* church, halfway up the ascent to the abbey. Built during the fifteenth and sixteenth centuries, it is dedicated to Saint Peter, keeper of the gates of heaven – for souls who have been weighed by the Archangel – and also patron saint of fishermen. There can thus be no doubt that it was for the villagers, who for centuries gained their livelihood from the sea, that the church was built. Looking very much like other small granite churches of the Cotentin peninsula, such as Saint-Pierre Langers near Sartilly, it is clearly distinguished by its function from the other buildings intended for the devotions of monks* and pilgrims.

The church nevertheless has links with the pilgrimage* route. A tremendous accumulation of ornaments, tapers and statues crowds the walls, and in front of a silver statue of Saint Michael lies an open book in which, every month, hundreds of visitors enter their prayers and petitions. Now that the conventual buildings* and abbey church* are visited principally as masterpieces of architecture, it is possible that, by a curious twist of fate, the parish church has become the last place of popular pilgrimage on the Mont. AG

Overleaf:
Paul Huard,
*Mont-Saint-Michel seen from the Port of Moidrey, c.*1840.
Oil on canvas.
Musée
d'Avranches.

Statuette of a pilgrim, sixteenth century. Limestone. Musée d'Avranches.

■ Pilgrimages

Going on pilgrimage was a typically medieval occupation (see Middle Ages). In essence it was an act of spiritual renewal, a temporary respite from belongings, relationships and routines which was intended to bring the pilgrim closer to God, following the teaching of Christ to his disciples: 'Take nothing for your journey, neither staves, nor scrip ... neither shoes ... nor money'. In the Middle Ages, each pilgrimage had its specific purpose. Pilgrims went to Santiago de Compostela in order to venerate the tomb of Saint James, one of the earliest witnesses of Christ, and to Rome to worship at the shrine of Saint Peter, the foundation stone of the Church, while in the Holy Land they could follow in the footsteps of Christ himself.

Pilgrims to the Mont, meanwhile, known as 'Miquelots', travelled there to draw inspiration from Michael the Archangel, the supreme champion of good, to marvel at his exploits and to draw the spiritual strength to engage in the same struggle. Others came to seek counsel from Saint Michael the weigher of souls, the arbiter of good and evil, the final advocate at the Last Judgement. Strange as it may seem to us today, such considerations were a compelling motive force in the Middle Ages, drawing most of the kings of France along the hallowed pilgrim routes to pray to the Archangel, protector of the kingdom (see Royal Visits). Walking beside them might have been those condemned to go on pilgrimage as a penance, children, the curious, criminals or bands of false pilgrims attempting to infiltrate the abbey on behalf of enemy forces (see Wars of Religion). GG

■ Polders

The idea has a long pedigree: already by the end of the Middle Ages* dykes and enclosures had made possible the cultivation of a few acres of land reclaimed from the sea. Washed away by the changing course of the rivers flowing into the bay,* these polders were often short-lived. It was only after 1856 that the government decided to create polders in the area on a large scale, entrusting the application of the scheme to a private company.

With total disregard for the historic nature of the area, the Couesnon* was canalized, the causeway* was built and the Mont ceased to be an island; the 'peril of the sea' was consigned to history. Although the initial plan – which failed to take into account the instability of offshore sedimentary deposits – was never fully implemented, plots of land

reclaimed from the sea since the mid-nineteenth century add up to an area of 2,800 hectares. AG

Poulard (Mère)

Born in Nevers, Annette Boutiaut (1851-1931) became chambermaid to Mme Corroyer, wife of the architect* of the Historic Monuments Service commissioned to carry out the first restoration work on the Mont. Thus it was that she made the acquaintance of Victor Poulard (1848-1924), eldest son of the baker on the Mont. Annette and Victor married in 1873, and opened a hotel in the village street.

The causeway* had not yet been built, and travellers arrived only when the sands could be crossed with safety. Guests were therefore often in a hurry to be served, and Annette would quickly make them one of her delicious omelettes. The hotel prospered, and soon it was attracting many famous names from the worlds of politics, the arts and literature.

In 1906 Victor and Annette retired. They are buried in the little cemetery on the Mont, where their epitaph reads: 'Here lie Victor and Annette Poulard, a faithful couple and generous hosts. May God receive them as they welcomed their guests.' HD

Polders in the bay of Mont-Saint-Michel.

Mère Poulard cooking one of her omelettes, c.1900.

◼ Priory

Placed under the authority of a mother house, a priory is a small monastery governed by a prior. In the thirteenth century the Mont-Saint-Michel possessed at least twenty of them. Some, such as Brion, Tombelaine,* Chausey* and Mont-Dol,* were retreat houses to which monks* could withdraw for meditation and prayer. Others, such as Saint-Broladre, were pious foundations or chantries, endowed by benefactors in return for continual prayers on their behalf. And lastly others, such as Ardevon, were set up to help manage the estate. Most of these lay along the coast, from Granville to Cancale, where most of the abbey's estates were concentrated. From the thirteenth century the abbots reduced the number of priories and handed over the running of the estates to more experienced secular administrators. HD

◼ Prison

From the time of the Ancien Régime the dungeons* on the Mont had made the 'Bastille of the sea' notorious. At the Revolution political prisoners were incarcerated on what was then known as Mont-Michel, and later Mont-Libre (Mount Freedom). Most of these were priests who had refused to swear the oath of civil constitu-

Chouan Prisoners on 'Mount Freedom', late nineteenth century. Musée d'Avranches.

tion of clergy, by which the Church was subordinated to the Republic: by 1793 they numbered 300, including Louis-Georges de Gouvetz, a canon from Avranches who belonged to one of the oldest families in the region, and whose ancestors included a chamberlain to Robert of Normandy and one of Saint Louis' crusader knights. On his release from the Mont, he secretly continued his mission at the height of the Terror, only to die at the bayonets of republican soldiers, in 1795, while ministering the last rites to a dying man. He is commemorated a few kilometres inland from Mont-Saint-Michel at Le Petit-Celland by a granite cross. In the nineteenth century the abbey buildings suffered devastat-

ing damage – as did Fontevraud at about the same time – when they were turned into a high security prison which quickly acquired a reputation for great harshness. The July Monarchy sent a considerable number of political detainees here, allowing them some concessions, such as individual cells, books, and the right to receive visitors. The republicans Armand Barbès (1809-70) and Auguste Blanqui (1805-81) were also brought here after the insurrection of 12 May 1839. In 1863, despite pleas from the villagers whose livelihood depended on it, the prison was closed down by Napoleon III, having been the focus of life on the Mont for nearly a century. The time of the architect* historians had come. AG

Ardevon Priory (Manche).

present vaulting being a mid-twelfth-century addition following damage by collapse and fire. This is the earliest example of Gothic* technique on the Mont. Thick and perhaps rather clumsy, the ribs are nevertheless a powerful demonstration of the principle later to be perfected by architects intent, as recommended by Suger, on making the 'entire church resplendent with marvellous unhindered light admitted by the most luminous of windows'. GG

■ Quicksands

Under certain conditions and in certain places, the silt of the bay* can turn into quicksand, caused when water evaporates from the surface, creating a firm layer over soft, water-logged silt. Walking on quicksand feels like stepping onto a sprung mattress – local fishermen call it 'sprung sand' – and only by moving quickly can the unfortunate walker avoid breaking the surface layer and being sucked down.

In a chapter of *Les Misérables* entitled 'With sand and women a certain fineness spells treachery', Victor Hugo describes a terrifying scene in which the quicksands claim their victim, which has probably helped to exaggerate their dangers. Such accidents are fortunately not common: even greater dangers are posed by sudden sea fogs and, above all, the speed of the incoming sea at high tide.* HD

Promenoir
des Moines
(Monks' Gallery)

36 Promenoir des Moines (Monks' Gallery)

The Promenoir des Moines, or Monks' Gallery, lies on the north side of the Mont, halfway up the Romanesque* monastery. Built over the Aquilon Chamber,* it supports the dormitory.* Although there is no doubt that it formed part of the cloister, its purpose is not clearly understood (see Chapter House).

This fine chamber comprises two parallel vaulted aisles separated by a row of small pillars. Its wide north wall has few windows, while the south side is cut partly out of the solid rock. Unusually, this otherwise Romanesque chamber has rib vaulting;* in fact only the lower part of the room is original, the

Paul Capellani,
*Victim of the
Quicksands at the
Mont-Saint-
Michel.* Plaster.
Musée du Mont-
Saint-Michel.

▪ Ramparts

The ramparts protecting the village* are a remarkable example of fifteenth-century military architecture. Constructed mostly during the Hundred Years War,* they were designed to take into account new developments in warfare as a result of the recent introduction of the cannon.

Until that time, ramparts had needed to be very high and reinforced by towers that were even higher. The Tour du Nord (North Tower) [11], which dates back to the thirteenth or fourteenth century, is typical of this older concept of defence: in order to capture this circular fortification perched on a sheer rock, the enemy would have had to scale the walls or undermine them.

In the new era of warfare, towers and curtain walls were kept fairly low so as to offer a smaller target for artillery. They were of uniform height, and communication between them was by means of a covered way; the garrison could thus quickly be deployed to the most vulnerable points.

A parapet resting on corbelled machicolations crowned both towers and walls. From here the defenders could launch missiles at the assailants, the foot of the wall sloping outwards to deflect falling objects towards the enemy.

To improve flanking fire the design of the towers was also modified. The Arcade Tower – the only tower to have retained its original roof timbers – and its neighbour the Tour du Roi (see King's Gate and Tower), both conform to the traditional circular plan. By contrast the Béatrix Tower [7], also known as the Tour de la Liberté, is horseshoe-shaped, allowing a wider field of fire.

Even more innovatory is the Boucle Tower [10] of 1481, its pentagonal layout, with no blind angles for defensive fire, anticipating the fortifications of

Vauban. Another novelty was the central chimney to allow smoke from cannon-fire to escape. The two other towers are of less interest. The Chollet Tower [9], or 'Half-Moon' Tower, guarded a postern gate which is now blocked up. The eighteenth-century Basse Tower [8] replaced an older bastion shown in ruins on the model.* HD

Ramparts near the Boucle Tower.

▪ Restoration. See Architects

Apparently reaching up to the sky, forty metres above the rock, the monks' refectory (thirty-four metres long and ten metres wide) nevertheless lies on the same level as the abbey church* and the cloister.* For practical reasons, the monks' kitchen lay beside it, at the same level. A vertical hoist and spiral stairway (the Corbins Tower) to the ground floor complete the arrangements for service and access.

To emphasize the communal nature of meals taken here, the architect has preferred not to divide the room in two with a central row of pillars – a sound decision as the single uninterrupted space is breathtaking, but one which entailed severe technical difficulties. The enormous timber roof, with no intermediate support, rests solely on the outer walls, which had to be reinforced until they were massively strong with no vulnerable points. As a dining hall, however, the room required plenty of light. Reconciling these conflicting requirements

seemed an impossible task. The solution was the brilliantly conceived 'wall of light', a cellular construction of thin but deep parallel piers between which the greatest possible amount of light is admitted. It is at once massive, relatively light in weight, and astonishingly luminous. Invisible from the entrance to the room, these unusual vertical windows

diffuse an indirect light which reaches as far as the reader's lectern. The spartan quality of this great space now appears as a virtue, but in the thirteenth century it would have had polychrome decorations, with painted ceiling and walls, stained glass windows and colourful glazed terracotta floor tiles similar to those of the guest chamber.*

Benedictine meals brought all the monks* together as a family. Three tables were set out in a U-shape along the walls, with the abbot, as father of the family, presiding at the end table. In the centre of the room was a table reserved for guests. During the meal, eaten in silence, a reading would be given from the lectern, amplified by the fine acoustics of the chamber. GG

Construction of
a rib vault.
AB - CD: Archivolt,
formeret or wall ribs.
BD: Transverse rib.
AD - BC: Diagonal
ribs. E: Keystone

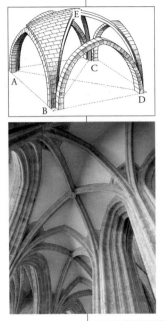

■ RIB VAULTING
A stone skeleton

With their tremendous accumulated experience, the monk-builders became the undisputed masters of the dynamics of vaulting. At Saint-Denis in the mid-twelfth century, the great Benedictine* architect Suger imagined fabulous possibilities for architecture, opened up by the introduction of rib vaulting. Henceforward the temples of the Lord were to become dazzling shrines of light.

Rib vaulting is the fundamental element in the technique of Gothic architecture.* Two diagonally intersecting arches collect and channel the downward and outward thrusts from the crown of the vault, redistributing them to four precise points were the intersecting stone ribs rest on stone pillars. This is the basic skeleton which secures the structure of the building, bearing the weight of the vault, bracing the walls, and allowing the introduction of windows at will. The system requires additional support on the outside of the building in the form of buttresses or flying buttresses – essential to counteract the lateral thrust of the arches. Rib vaulting is completed by the addition of transverse and wall ribs.

The flexibility of the system was infinite, making it equally suitable not only for perfect squares, but also for rectangular, triangular and circular plans (see Promenoir). GG

Abbey church,
detail of vaulting
in the ambulatory.

25 Robert de Torigni

Robert de Torigni was prior of Le Bec-Helloüin when the monks* of Mont-Saint-Michel elected him as their abbot in 1154. Henry II of England, Duke of Normandy, was happy to ratify his election and was to be his guest on three occasions, notably in 1158 in the company of the French king Louis VII. Robert exercised a strong spiritual influence over his monastery, which soon numbered some sixty monks – a number never equalled since. Trained at the school of Bec, one of the most brilliant in western Christendom, he raised the scriptorium* of the Mont to an outstanding level of excellence. He is said to

Opposite:
Abbey church,
south-west pillar
of the transept
crossing.

have enriched the library with 140 manuscripts,* earning the Mont the name 'city of books'. He himself wrote a history entitled *Annales* and a chronicle of the dukes of Normandy.*

He was also a fine administrator, recovering property pillaged from the abbey and increasing its estates through purchases, exchanges and donations. As a result, he was able to undertake new building works, most of which have now disappeared, with the exception of the building to the west which housed the judicial services, and the abbot's lodgings. Having governed the abbey with authority and wisdom for more than thirty years, Robert died in 1186. HD

■ ROMANESQUE ARCHITECTURE
The European context

During the eleventh century the rise of powerful dynasties such as the Ottonian, Capetian and Norman, the reforms stimulated by the Cluniac monasteries and the growth in popularity of pilgrimages to both Compostela and Mont-Saint-Michel conspired to encourage new building, and with it new developments in architecture.

The Romanesque church consisted of a combination of complex forms, frequently focused on a central crossing and tower, with varying treatments of the chevet: with a three-apse plan as at Bernay, or with an ambulatory with or without radiating chapels, as at Rouen or the original chancel at Mont-Saint-Michel. A new concept of the nature of the supporting structure, involving composite pillars and walls articulated in a series of bays by half-columns, served to receive the weight of the vaulting. Groined and barrel vaulting now became increasingly popular, and by the late eleventh century Norman architects were erecting the first rib vaults* at Lessay and Durham.

It was against this background that the Romanesque abbey on Mont-Saint-Michel was built, laid out around an abbey church* which itself was erected on top of a series of underground Romanesque constructions: Notre-Dame-sous-Terre,* the vaulted crypts* under the transepts, and the crypt lying beneath the chevet – replaced by the Crypte des Gros Piliers in the Gothic* period.

The kitchens, the infirmary,* and the dormitory* adjoining the northern side of the nave and rebuilt after 1103, are essentially Romanesque, as is the Aquilon Chamber* with its ribbed vaulting and powerful transverse arches resting on a row of columns with capitals. The Promenoir,* or Monks' Gallery, at the transition between Romanesque and Gothic, displays advances in the technique of rib vaulting.* In the village* the parish church* is also a Romanesque foundation, later rebuilt. MB

■ Royal Visits

Even before the start of the Hundred Years War* the Mont had a special significance for the French kings, who frequently came on pilgrimage* here. In 1158, Henry II of England came here for a solemn reconciliation with Louis VII (the 'Pious'). In 1256, Saint Louis, visited and endowed the abbey, returning in 1264. His son Philippe III (the 'Bold'), also came on pilgrimage, followed by Philippe le Bel, who donated relics in 1311.

Visits by Charles VI – the mad king known as the 'Beloved' – in 1393 and 1394, by Marie of Anjou, wife of Charles VII, and by Louis XI in 1462, prior to his founding of the Order of Saint-Michel,* are further evidence of the Mont's popularity with the monarchy. Charles VIII came in 1487, Francois I in 1518 and 1532, and Charles IX in 1561, on the eve of the Wars of Religion.*

In exchange for spiritual protection, these royal visits were also a confirmation of dynastic continuity: for Francois I, who by birth had no claim to the throne, it was an opportunity to reclaim his Capetian lineage and his ultimate descent from Louis VII and Saint Louis. For successive abbots these visits provided the donations necessary for the completion of the abbey buildings. Following the first visit of Saint Louis, for example, the fortifications were improved. AG

35 Saint-Etienne (Chapel)

Dedicated to Saint Stephen, like one of the earliest Christian sanctuaries to be built on the Mont-Tombe,* this chapel was one of the new buildings undertaken by Robert de

The Chapel of Saint-Etienne.

Torigni* in the twelfth century, to be considerably altered in the following century. Originally it had a simple roof of exposed timbers with decorated panels, resting on a moulding which is still visible on the north wall. In the thirteenth century, the level of the floor was lowered and the timber roof was replaced by elegant rib vaulting.*

In its position between the infirmary* and cemetery (see Ossuary), it served as a mortuary chapel. In 1978 a late fifteenth-century Pietà was placed beneath the archway where once there stood a stone bath, used for washing the dead before they were buried in their monks' habits. HD

■ Saint Michael. See Michael

39 Scriptorium

See Knights' Chamber

■ SILTING IN THE BAY
'Mont-Saint-Michel must remain an island.' (Hugo)

For six thousand years the bay* of Mont-Saint-Michel has been the scene of recurring confrontations between sea and sand. The first takes place daily when, at ebb tide, thousands of cubic metres of silt from the river and the sea are left to form the *tangue* of the bay. The second struggle has been played out over a longer time-scale, with the bay being alternately silted up and then flooded again by a rapid rise in the level of the ocean. The third conflict is dictated by the geography of the bay, which acts as a funnel between the coasts of the Cotentin peninsula and Brittany. At high tide a tremendous volume of water surges into it, raising the sea level by as much as fifteen metres. At the funnel's narrowest point the sea forces its way up the coastal rivers, raising their water levels considerably. When the tide recedes again this gigantic reservoir empties in a few hours, at a rate of flow comparable to that of the Volga, flushing the sands of the bay out to sea.

In the Middle Ages human agencies entered the struggle. The results of early attempts to reclaim cultivable land were modest, but in 1865 an ambitious programme of land reclamation (see Polders) was embarked upon, based on one fundamental principle: the accumulation of deposits of sand and silt, to stem the flow of these mighty currents once and for all. A century later, the shoreline has advanced by six kilometres, and grass is spreading on the dunes. GG

The bay before 1856.

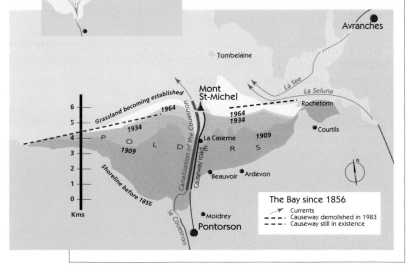

Avranches

Tombelaine

Mont St-Michel

La See

La Selune

Rochetorin

Grassland becoming established

1964

1964
1934

Canalization of the Couesnon

Causeway road

La Caserne

1909

Courtils

1934

P O L D E R S

1909

Shoreline before 1856

Beauvoir   Ardevon

N

Moidrey

le Couesnon

Pontorson

The Bay since 1856
⟋ Currents
– – – Causeway demolished in 1983
– – – Causeway still in existence

■ STEEPLE

During the second quarter of the twelfth century, Abbot Bernard du Bec built a tower over the central crossing of the transept of the abbey church, which was to be crowned with a number of different steeples. The only early example of which we can form a precise picture is depicted in a miniature of about 1390, painted by one of the Limbourg Brothers for the *Très Riches Heures du Duc de Berry*. If this steeple managed

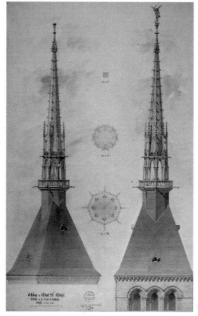

Victor Petitgrand, *Abbey Church of Mont-Saint-Michel: steeple of the central tower*, 1895. Watercoloured drawing. Paris, Bibliothèque du Patrimoine.

to survive the collapse of the chancel* in 1421, it had certainly disappeared by about 1500, when lightning set fire* to the building. In 1509, Abbot Guillaume de Lamps erected a new steeple, seemingly crowned with a gilded statue of the Archangel. This slender wooden spire, of which we have a description by a late sixteenth-century historian, succumbed to another fire caused by lightning in 1594. It was replaced by the 'imperial dome' with a squat bell tower shown on the model of 1701. This too burned down, in 1776, to be replaced in its turn by a hipped roof, the ridges of which were removed in 1796 in order to accommodate a relay platform for Chappe's recently invented aerial telegraph, linking Paris with Saint-Malo. The Mont had to wait for the restorations of the late nineteenth century before it regained its tall, slender outline with a steeple, the work of the architect* Victor Petitgrand between 1893 and 1897.

Petitgrand's first task was to rebuild the transept crossing in neo-Romanesque style, correcting the distortions perpetrated since 1421, followed by the tower surmounting it. This was topped by a wooden steeple covered with embossed bronze, which in turn was crowned on 6 August 1897 with a statue of the Archangel, bringing the steeple's total height to just under 160 metres above the bay. The gilt bronze sculpture by Emmanuel Frémiet* is four and a half metres high and weighs 500 kilograms.

Petitgrand has been accused of erecting an imitation of the spire designed by Viollet-le-Duc* for Notre-Dame in Paris. While his steeple is not on the scale of that shown in the miniature of the *Très Riches Heures du Duc de Berry,* it nevertheless has the great virtue of endowing the Mont's silhouette with a powerful verticality combined with a considerable degree of elegance. HD

30 Storeroom

Situated on the ground floor of the western part of the Merveille,* the storeroom supports both the Knights' Chamber* and the cloister.*

This massively built room was used to store food on a scale sufficient to supply the large numbers of regular meals required as well as the unpredictable needs of those arriving on pilgrimage.* The groined vaulting of exquisite simplicity is supported by square pillars without capitals, while the tremendously thick walls are pierced occasionally by narrow windows. Provisions and sometimes building materials were brought into the room through an opening on the north side, equipped with a hoist similar in principle to the great wheel.* Supplies were stored in this huge, dark space, cool and well ventilated, before being taken up to the kitchens above. The large vertical shaft of the medieval hoist can still be seen in place. GG

45 Terrasse du Saut-Gaultier

The Terrasse du Saut-Gaultier (Gaultier's Leap), at the summit of the Grand Degré,* is also known as 'Beauregard' or 'Miranda' because of the panorama which it affords of the southern part of the bay.*

Some writers have claimed that the Gaultier of the terrace's most popular name was a sixteenth-century sculptor imprisoned in the abbey, who threw himself off the platform in despair. In fact the origins of the name, which go back to at least the thirteenth century, are more romantic, for it is said to commemorate another Gaultier, who hurled himself from the pinnacle of a high rock in order to prove his love for a woman.

Opening on to the terrace is the church portal, dating from the thirteenth century. In 1862 its tympanum was embellished with a bas-relief by Barré depicting Saint Aubert's vision of Saint Michael, now to be seen in the porch at the entrance to the Merveille.* HD

■ TIDES: AS FAST AS A GALLOPING HORSE?

The bay* of Mont-Saint-Michel is witness to the strongest tides in Europe, which at their most extreme can leave a difference of over fifteen metres between high and low tide levels.

As the sands are almost completely flat, the sea retreats by as much as twenty kilometres at low tide, only to return, so they say, 'at the speed of a galloping horse'. The average speed of the returning tide is in fact 3.750 kilometres per hour, which is already considerable; in some places, however, especially when driven by a strong westerly wing, it can reach speeds of as much as twenty-five to thirty kilometres per hour. Over the centuries, countless pilgrims, and more recently walkers, have been caught by the incoming tide and drowned. For this reason it is imperative to find out the time of the returning tide before venturing out on to the sands.

When high water reaches the estuaries of the small rivers which flow into the bay, it pushes back their weaker currents to form waves between fifty centimetres and a metre high. Equivalent to the tidal bores on the Gironde and the Seine, these are known locally as *barres de mer*. As the receding tide is not as strong as the incoming tide, much of the sediment carried by the sea is unfortunately deposited to become the main cause of silting* in the bay. HD

The Marquis of Tombelaine (1854-92).

■ Tombelaine

The islet of Tombelaine, rising from the vastness of the bay* three kilometres offshore and inaccessible except on foot, is a reminder of what the Mont must have been like before the first sanctuary was established there. The best view of this islet, which for many years served as a stopping-off place for pilgrims, is from the far side of the Mont. Now deserted, Tombelaine once had its own buildings. In 1137, Bernard du Bec, abbot of the Mont, founded a priory* on the rock – despite its lack of water supply – to which the monks would go on retreat. Travellers were also received there. When the Mont was besieged during the Hundred Years War,* from 1442, the English fortified the islet with a citadel which survived for centuries. It was repaired by Fouquet, Louis XIV's all-powerful finance minister, who included among his titles 'Governor of Mont-Saint-Michel, Tombelaine and the Islands'; five years after his disgrace in 1661, the king, fearing that Fouquet might use his coastal fortresses as a personal power-base, had Tombelaine's defences razed to the ground.

Reverting to the role suggested by its original name, meaning 'tomb' or 'tumulus', the rock henceforth formed a sombre counterpart to the radiant and hallowed Merveille* opposite. A wilderness once more (though there were plans in the 1930s to build a 'panoramic palace' with a Gothic casino), it became a refuge for scallop fishers, who were ruled at the turn of the century by a strange character, part-hermit part-peasant, known as the Marquis of Tombelaine. His photograph can still be seen on old postcards. AG

■ TOURISM: THE HUMAN TIDE

With over two and a half million visitors from around the world each year, Mont-Saint-Michel is one of the most popular monuments in France – a phenomenon which began only in the late nineteenth century, when the dismal prison* was at last revealed as a masterpiece of medieval art, its former splendour regained thanks to the efforts of the architects* who worked there.

The annual pilgrimage* held on the feast day of Saint Michael still attracts a number of the faithful. Although it goes back to the end of the nineteenth century – when pilgrims began to be attracted more by miracles than by relics – it is only of relatively minor importance nowadays. Nevertheless, the majority of visitors tour not only the village* and the site but also visit the buildings of the Merveille.* Sadly, the great majority of these huge numbers come on day trips to the Mont alone, thus missing out on all the many other wonders – of art, architecture and landscape – to be found in the surrounding areas of Brittany and Normandy. AG

■ UNESCO
A world heritage site

'One of the wonders of the western world', or the 'eighth wonder of the modern world': the epithets applied to the Mont tend to link it to the Great Pyramid, that wonder of the ancient world whose silhouette it seems to echo. The Mont-Saint-Michel, which – as Hugo put it in *Quatre-vingt-treize* – 'is to the ocean what the pyramid of Cheops is to the desert', has since 1984 been listed by UNESCO as a world heritage site, along with other outstanding spiritual centres as varied as the Taj Mahal, the Inca temple at Machu Picchu, Borobudur in Indonesia, Persepolis in Iran, the Monastery of the Hieronymites of Belem in Portugal and the Campo dei Miracoli in Pisa. This international classification, of vital significance for sites under threat such as Angkor in Cambodia, has had little practical impact on the Mont-Saint-Michel, which is already heavily protected by French legislation concerning historic monuments.* It has, however, served to alert international public opinion to the dangers of silting,* and has added weight to arguments calling for the removal of the causeway.* AG

■ Village

Huddled between the ramparts* and the abbey, the village has always tended to turn to commerce* for its livelihood. The inhabitants who settled on the rock from the tenth century undoubtedly included fishermen, but the majority of them sold souvenirs or kept inns, their prosperity rising and falling with the Mont's reputation as a place of pilgrimage.*

The village has its own parish church* dedicated to the apostle Peter. Until 1789, the villagers were feudal subjects of the abbey, which had powers to 'order and constrain' and to administer justice. With the Revolution the village gained its freedom, becoming a commune administered by a mayor. The single village street is now lined with thriving businesses. Many of the houses were rebuilt during the Belle Epoque in response to the beginnings of modern tourism,* but a few fifteenth- and sixteenth-century examples have survived. Of particular interest are the Hôtellerie de la Lycorne and its annex, the Maison de l'Artichaut [6], which straddles the road; the fine half-timbered Auberge de la Sirène; and the old communal bread oven with its façade supported by two granite arches. HD

La Maison de l'Artichaut.

Viollet-le-Duc

Eugène-Emmanuel Viollet-le-Duc (1815-79) stayed only once on the Mont-Saint-Michel, from 29 May to 8 June 1835. He was instantly captivated by the place, writing to his father: 'We have been settled here on the Mont-Saint-Michel since yesterday morning. It is as frightfully cold and windy as in the month of March. Despite all that – Vive le Mont-Saint-Michel! No place could be more beautiful or savage, nowhere more grandiose or melancholy.'

During his stay he made innumerable drawings and paintings which, rather than mere objective records, are works of great sensitivity and technical mastery.

Eugène-Emmanuel Viollet-le-Duc, by Félix Nadar, 1878.

Eugène-Emmanuel Viollet-le-Duc, *La Crypte des Gros Piliers*, 1835. Watercolour on ivory paper. Private collection.

Overleaf:
Aerial view of the west terrace and abbey church.

He never forgot the abbey, which he included in his *Dictionnaire raisonné of French Architecture from the Eleventh to the Sixteenth Century* under the entries for 'monastic architecture' and 'cloister'.*

He was not commissioned to restore the buildings on the Mont, despite the hopes expressed in 1868 by Mgr Bravard, Bishop of Coutances and Avranches, and by the prefect of the *département* of La Manche; it was at his instigation, however, that the work was entrusted in 1872 to Edouard Corroyer (see Architects). HD

Wars of Religion

Having triumphantly survived the Hundred Years War,* the Mont once more served as a fortress in the sixteenth century, during the Wars of Religion. It was here that the League, made up of Catholics loyal to the king, withstood the assaults of the Protestant faction, led by Gabriel de Montgomery – who had accidentally killed Henri II in a tournament in 1559. Pontorson, opposite the Mount, became a bridgehead for the Huguenots.

The Mont's defences came close to being breached on a number of occasions. In 1577, a score of soldiers disguised as pilgrims tried to capture it before giving themselves up. In 1589 the same trick was tried again, and in 1591 an armed band of Protestants who had managed to infiltrate the abbey were slaughtered on the spot. The region around Avranches was to remain a bastion of Protestantism long after the signing of the Edict of Nantes by Henri IV in 1598. AG

Watch-dogs

Like Saint-Malo, the nearby seafaring town whose arms are supported by two heraldic dogs, the Mont-Saint-Michel was for centuries guarded by mastiffs. It was probably at the time of the English blockade of the Hundred Years War* that the garrison acquired a pack of watch-dogs which were let loose on the ramparts* at night. So celebrated did they become that Louis XI, on a visit to the Mont in 1470 (see Royal Visits), bestowed a grant in perpetuity for their upkeep. Their use was discontinued only in the seventeenth century. AG

47 West Terrace

From this platform which serves as a parvis to the abbey church* there is a superb view out over the bay,* from the Pointe du Grouin in Brittany to the Pointe de Carolles in Normandy, with small coastal rivers such as the Couesnon* meandering across immensities of sand. Both sands and sea constantly change colour, reflecting the sky like a great mirror. To the south-west the land is chequered with rows of trees planted along dykes built to protect the polders.* Mont-Dol* rises twenty kilometres away, due west of the abbey church. Three kilometres to the north, Tombelaine* emerges from the sands, to be completely cut off at high tide. In clear weather the Isles of Chausey* can be made out far away on the horizon.

The terrace was considerably enlarged after the fire* of 1776, which obliged the monks to pull down the first three bays of the nave of the abbey church, as well as two-thirds of the dormitory* adjoining the

north aisle. The original foundations of the abbey church, of the eleventh-century façade and of the towers which were added in the twelfth century, were marked on the terrace by means of different ground levels when the pavement was restored in 1963. The architect* Yves-Marie Froidevaux also commissioned two tombstones to commemorate Robert de Torigni* and his successor Martin de Furmendi, both buried near the Romanesque porch.

The church's present façade, added in 1780, has a very simple design – two tiers of columns surmounted by a triangular pediment – which harmonizes relatively successfully with the Romanesque architecture of the rest of the building. HD

34 Wheel (Great)

Constructed in the nineteenth century when the abbey became a prison,* the great wheel operates according to exactly the same principle as the treadwheels used on the great construction sites of the Middle Ages and as far back as antiquity.

As the six prisoners placed inside the wheel walked forward it would turn, drawing up a rope which wound round the axle. The rope stretched down outside the building as far as the road, where the other end was attached to a trolley on rollers, which was then drawn back and forth along a stone ramp, hauling loads of up to two tonnes. Medieval equivalents, known as *poulains,* were generally much smaller, and were operated by one or two workmen. A few examples still exist in Europe today. GG

William the Conqueror

In 1064, William the Bastard – not yet the Conqueror – came to the Mont, an event clearly depicted on the tapestry later commissioned by his half-brother Odo of Conteville, now known as the Bayeux Tapestry. William, in the company of Harold – not yet his sworn enemy nor his rival for the English throne – is shown leading an expedition past the Mont-Saint-Michel on their way to Brittany.* Soldiers can be seen fording the Couesnon,* while some of the horses lose their footing in the sands.

The lower border is filled with examples of the fauna and flora* of the bay,* and the scene is dominated by the Mont, with the crosses on its

Bayeux Tapestry (detail): *William and Harold crossing the Couesnon, c.*1095. Bayeux, Musée de la Tapisserie.

summit touching the sky. It is possible that this architectural ensemble is a representation of the Romanesque narthex or porch through which visitors would have entered the original abbey church.* The inclusion of the rock of the Archangel in the tapestry is an indication of the strategic and symbolic importance of the site in the eleventh century.

After defeating Harold at Hastings in 1066 and becoming king of England himself, William appointed monks from Mont-Saint-Michel to head four English abbeys. AG

WRITERS AND FICTION
A fascinating colossus

From Madame de Sévigné in 1661 to the travellers of the romantic era, the Mont has been an inspiration to the writers who have visited it. Stendhal – rather indifferent – in 1837, Mérimée – conscientious – in 1841, and Flaubert in 1847, all undertook what was gradually to become a re-creation of a medieval pilgrimage, at a time when Hugo's *Notre-Dame de Paris* (*The Hunchback of Notre-Dame*) had done much to make gargoyles and capitals fashionable in France. In rediscovering the architecture of the Mont, however, the romantics had no choice but to look beyond the 'troubador' decor to the insalubrious, dilapidated and icy-cold prison that the abbey had become. When he travelled there with Juliette Drouet in 1836, Hugo was torn between admiration and horror.

As well as evoking the Mont in his celebrated *Horla*, Maupassant also devoted a novella to it, *The Legend of Mont-Saint-Michel*: 'I had first seen it from Cancale, this fairytale castle set in the sea [...] Solitary, the steep-sided abbey, thrust far out from the shore like a fantastic castle, mesmerizing like a palace in a dream, unbelievably strange and beautiful, remained almost black against the purple dawn.'

Paul Féval* made the Mont the setting of a series of popular novels, while the 1930s writer Roger Vercel dedicated his sentimental *Sous le pied de l'archange* to it. The local novelist Jean de la Varende adopted a lyrical, historical style in his *Mont-Saint-Michel* of 1943. And in making the Mont-Saint-Michel the setting for an episode of the adventures of Lefranc, *L'Ouragan de feu*, in 1975, the Belgian Jacques Martin turned it into the hero of a strip cartoon. AG

Victor Hugo, *Le Mont-Saint-Michel*. Ink and wash, Paris, Maison de Victor Hugo.

708 St Aubert, Bishop of Avranches, builds a shrine to Saint Michael tended by twelve canons.

867-8 Visit by the monk Bernard, the first known pilgrim.

911 Creation of the duchy of Normandy.

933 The dioceses of Coutances and Avranches become part of Normandy.

966 Benedictine monks from the abbey of St Wandrille at Fontenelle replace the canons installed by St Aubert.

992 The first fire starts in village houses and spreads to the abbey.

1007 Marriage on the Mont of Richard II Duke of Normandy and Judith of Brittany.

1023 Abbot Hildebert II starts construction of the Romanesque abbey church.

1048 Abbot Raoul de Beaumont builds the transept of the abbey church.

1063 Abbot Ranulphe de Bayeux begins work on the nave.

1065 William the Bastard, Duke of Normandy, crosses the Couesnon with Harold before an expedition into Brittany.

1066 Conquest of England by William, henceforth known as the 'Conqueror'.

1091 Henry I, 'Beauclerc', youngest son of William the Conqueror, takes refuge on the Mont, where he is besieged by his two brothers, William Rufus and Robert 'Curthose'.

1103 North side of nave of abbey church collapses.

1112 Good Friday, 22 April: outbreak of fire caused by lightning.

1136 Central tower of abbey church built by Abbot Bernard du Bec.

1138 August: fire started by people of Avranches; only the abbey church left undamaged.

1154 Election of Robert de Torigni, the Mont's greatest abbot.

1158 Meeting on the Mont of Louis VII of France and Henry II of England.

1166 Henry II Plantagenet visits the Mont again.

1172 Reconciliation of Henry II with the church, in the cathedral of Avranches, after the assassination of Thomas Becket.

1186 Death of Robert de Torigni.

1204 Normandy becomes part of France; Guy de Thouars, ally of Philippe Auguste, sets fire to the Mont.

1210 Founding in Paris by Philippe Auguste of the Confraternity of Saint-Michel-de-la-Mer.

1211 Construction of the 'Merveille' started.

1228 Completion of cloister.

1256 Pilgrimage of Saint Louis.

1264 Second pilgrimage of Saint Louis.

1272 Pilgrimage of thanksgiving by King Philippe III the 'Bold' after escaping the plague at the siege of Tunis.

1300 13 July: fire caused by lightning destroys the tower of the abbey church and almost all the houses in the village.

1311 Pilgrimage of Philippe le Bel.

1333 Pilgrimage of the 'Pastoureaux'.

1337 Hundred Years War begins.

1350 Lightning again causes fire.

1357 Abbot Nicolas le Vitrier appointed captain of the garrison by the Dauphin Charles.

1365 Bertrand Du Guesclin installs his wife Tiphaine de Gaguenel on the Mont.

1374 8 July: outbreak of fire caused by lightning.

1393 Pilgrimage of King Charles VI.

1394 Second pilgrimage of Charles VI, who chooses Abbot Pierre Le Roy as privy councillor.

1410 Death in Bologna of Pierre Le Roy, councillor to Pope Alexander V.

1417 His successor, Robert Jolivet, fortifies the village.

1420 Abbot Jolivet defects to the English.

1421 Collapse of Romanesque chancel of abbey church.

1424 Guided by Jolivet, English forces organize land and sea blockade of the Mont.

1425 Corsairs from Saint-Malo force the blockade.

1433 Second Monday after Easter: fire sweeps the village but apparently spares the abbey.

1434 Defenders of the Mont repel an English assault, capturing two cannon.

1446 Construction work started on the Crypte des Gros Piliers, supporting the Gothic chancel of the abbey church.

1447 Pilgrimage of Queen Marie of Anjou, wife of Charles VII.

1450 End of Hundred Years War in Normandy: the English abandon Tombelaine.

1462 Pilgrimage of Louis XI.

1467 Second pilgrimage of Louis XI.

1469 Louis XI founds the Order of the Knights of Saint-Michel at Amboise.

1472 Third pilgrimage of Louis XI; the king has an iron cage installed in the Romanesque part of the abbey to hold a number of unfortunate prisoners.

1488 Pilgrimage of King Charles VIII.

1509 Fire caused by lightning necessitates rebuilding of the steeple of the abbey church by Guillaume de Lamps.

1518 Pilgrimage of François I.

1523 Completion of the chancel of the abbey church by Abbot Jean de Lamps.

1531 Second pilgrimage to the Mont by François I, who meets the Saint-Malo seafarer Jacques Cartier.

1562 Pilgrimage of Charles IX, last French king to visit the Mont. Beginning of Wars of Religion.

1577 Protestant reformers make unsuccessful attempt to capture the abbey.

1589 Second attempt by Protestants under Montgomery also fails.

1591 Montgomery's forces fail in final attempt to capture the abbey.

1594 23 May: fire caused by lightning. The steeple and timbers of the chancel of the abbey church burn.

1598 Edict of Nantes ends Wars of Religion.

1615 An infant just over a year old, Henri II of Lorraine, named as commendatary abbot of the Mont.

1622 Maurist reforms introduced.

1661 Fortifications on Tombelaine razed following the disgrace of former governor, the 'surintendant' Fouquet.

1776 16 August: nave of the abbey church damaged by fire.

1790 Departure of the Benedictine monks.

1793 Three hundred priests refusing to accept the civil constitution of clergy imprisoned in the abbey.

1811 The abbey becomes a high security prison.

1818 Collapse of lodgings built by Robert de Torigni.

1830 Legitimist and republican political detainees imprisoned in abbey lodgings.

1834 22-3 October: fire breaks out in straw hat-making workshops in the abbey church.

1835 Visit of Viollet-le-Duc.

1836 Visit of Victor Hugo.

1839 Blanqui, Barbès and other republicans imprisoned on the Mont.

1863 The prison is closed down.

1865-86 The abbey is rented by the Bishop of Coutances and Avranches to house diocesan missionaries.

1872 Edouard Corroyer put in charge of restoring the abbey.

1874 The abbey classified as a historic monument.

1877-9 Construction of the causeway to the Mont.

1897 Completion of the steeple designed by Victor Petitgrand.

1959 Excavations of Yves-Marie Froidevaux uncover Notre-Dame-sous-Terre.

1965-6 Commemoration of the millenary of the monastic foundation by monks from St Wandrille and Le Bec Hellouin.

1969 A new religious community established on the Mont.

1984 The Mont classified as a world heritage site by UNESCO.

S E L E C T   B I B L I O G R A P H Y

Dom Thomas Leroy, *Les Curieuses recherches du Mont-Saint-Michel*, 2 vol., Caen 1877.

Dom Jean Huynes, *Histoire générale de l'abbaye du Mont-Saint-Michel*, 2 vol., Rouen, 1877-8.

Paul Gout, *Le Mont-Saint-Michel. Histoire de l'abbaye et de la ville. Étude archéologique et architecturale des monuments*, 2 vol., Paris, 1910.

Germain Bazin, *Le Mont-Saint-Michel. Histoire et archéologie des origines à nos jours*, nouv. éd., New York, 1978.

Gérard Guillier, *Nous avons bâti le Mont-Saint-Michel*, Rennes, 1978.

Henry Decaëns, *La Belle époque au Mont-Saint-Michel*, Rennes, 1985.

Millénaire monastique du Mont-Saint-Michel, 5 vol., TOME 1 : *Histoire et vie monastiques*, edited by Dom Jean Laporte, Paris, 1966. TOME 2 : *Vie montoise et rayonnement intellectuel*, edited by Raymonde Foreville, Paris, 1967. TOME 3 : *Culte de saint Michel et pèlerinages au Mont*, edited by Marcel Baudot, Paris, 1971. TOME 4 : *Bibliographie générale et sources*, by Michel Nortier, Paris, 1967. TOME 5 : *Études archéologiques*, edited by Michel Nortier, Paris, 1993.

I N D E X

USEFUL INFORMATION

Tourist office: Tel: (16) 33 60 14 30

Mont-Saint-Michel :
Open daily throughout the year.

The abbey:
Open daily except 1 January, 1 May, 1
and 11 November and 25 December.
• Guided tours lasting one hour (in French,
English and, in summer, German and Italian);
lecture-tours lasting two hours, in French. For
details telephone (16) 33 60 04 52
• *Son et lumière, Les Imaginaires:* daily except
Sundays 15 May-29 September, 10pm-1am (last
admission at midnight), 9pm-midnight during
September.

Private museums in the village :
Open 9am-7pm in summer; 9.30 pm-4.30 am
out of season; closed 25 December.

Musée maritime:	Tel: (16) 33 60 14 09
Musée Grévin:	Tel: (16) 33 60 14 09
Archéoscope:	Tel: (16) 33 48 09 37
Logis Tiphaine:	Tel: (16) 33 60 23 34

Monastic community of Mont-Saint-Michel :
Tel: (16) 33 60 14 47

**For the pilgrimage centre
and Archiconfrérie of Saint-Michel,
contact the Presbytery of Mont-Saint-Michel:**
Tel: (16) 33 60 14 05

During the summer, guided walks are organized
in the bay and across the sands
For details contact
La Maison de la Baie: Tel: (16) 33 70 86 46

Times may be subject to alteration: visitors are advised to check in
advance.

Photographic acknowledgements: Archives Henri Decaëns 21, 40, 41, 52, 58-59b, 63, 97b, 108h, 112h ; Henri
Decaëns 10, 62h, 64-65, 78, 97h, 98-99 ; Marine Guillier 45 ; AIX-EN-PROVENCE, Jean Bernard 15, 16, 17, 32, 33,
34, 35, 36b, 38, 42h, 44, 46-47, 48, 50, 51, 53, 54, 59h, 61h, 69, 70, 71, 74-75, 82h, 84, 92, 93, 94-95, 100h, 104,
106-107, 110-111 ; AVRANCHES, Bibliothèque municipale 13, 14, 42b ; PARIS, Altitude/Yann Arthus-Bertrand cou-
verture, 12, 36-37h, 67 ; Bibliothèque nationale de France 109h ; Bulloz 24-25, 61b ; Jean-Loup Charmet 66, 82b ;
Daniel Chenot 28, 29, 30, 39b, 43, 72h, 80, 101, 108b ; C.N.M.H.S © Spadem 1996/Philippe Berthe 114/Daniel
Chenot 18-19, 20, 55, 56-57, 64h, 90-91/A. Wolf 68h/Lonchampt-Delehaye 68b, 96 ; Dagli Orti 27, 39h, 60 ;
Flammarion 22, 38b, 58h, 85, 87, 105 ; Roger-Viollet 65h, 72b, 115 ; VANVES, Explorer/L. Girard 31b/J-M Labat
102-103/E. Poupinet 112b.D. Repérant 113 Lauros-Giraudon 31h, 79, 89 ; Giraudon 4-5, 73, 77, 88.

Series Director: Stéphane GUÉGAN
Series editor: Béatrice PETIT
Editor: Barbara MELLOR
Art director: Frédéric CÉLESTIN
Plans by: Thierry RENARD
Designer: Frédéric VIGNALS
Photoengraving, Films: Pollina s.a., Luçon
Paper: BVS-Plus glossy 135 g. distributed by Axe Papier, Champigny-sur-Marne
Cover printed by Pollina s.a., Luçon
Printed and bound in June 1996 by Pollina s.a., Luçon

© 1996 Flammarion, Paris
ISBN : 2-08-011783-1
ISSN : 1258-2794
N° d'édition : 1197
N° d'impression : 70227
Dépôt légal : July 1996
Printed in France

Pages 4-5: Emmanuel Lansyer (1835-93), *The cloister of Mont-Saint-Michel* (detail).
Quimper, Musée des Beaux-Arts.